A SECRET WORLD
OF SEX

A SECRET WORLD OF SEX

Forbidden Fruit:
The British Experience 1900–1950

Steve Humphries

SIDGWICK & JACKSON
LONDON

For Sally

First published in Great Britain in 1988
by Sidgwick & Jackson Limited
First published in paperback 1991

Copyright © 1988 by Steve Humphries

Designed by Michael Head

ISBN 0-283-99750-8

Printed in Great Britain by
Butler & Tanner Limited
Frome, Somerset

Photoset by Rowland Phototypesetting Limited
Bury St Edmunds, Suffolk
for Sidgwick & Jackson Limited
Cavaye Place
London SW10 9PG

CONTENTS

PICTURE ACKNOWLEDGMENTS

The author and publisher gratefully acknowledge the following for supplying illustrations:

Gina Baker, 93; BBC Hulton Picture Library, 11, 17, 27, 29, 61, 72/3, 118, 125, 128, 139, 178, 179, 186, 195, 200, 203; Beamish Museum, 148; Dudley Cave 198; Church Army Archives, 20, 57, 64, 69, 88, 91, 135, 174, 175; Colindale Newspaper Library, 18, 44, 66, 68, 105, 127, 151, 177; Coventry City Libraries, 201; Monica Fawcett, 84; Ada Haskins, 14; Howarth-Loomes, 117, 134; Imperial War Museum, 74, 113, 213; Lord Jessel, 130; Lear's Magic Lanterns, 39, 54, 150, 197, 206; London Library, 143, 153, 155; Billie Love, 41, 49, 100, 102, 145, 168/9, 176, 189; The Photo Source, 24/5, 184/5; Pictorial Nostalgia Library, i, 32, 33, 45, 82, 96, 98, 133, 166, 167, 209, 210; Rev. C. Post, 21, 22; Scout Association, 52; Lady Marguerite Tangye, 36, 120/21, 131; Victoria & Albert Picture Library, 172; Wellcome Institute, 77, 111; Yorkshire Art Circus, 162/3.

ACKNOWLEDGMENTS

I have lots of debts of gratitude to all those who have helped in the making of this book. First, thanks to the many people who wrote to me, and especially to those who allowed me and my tape recorder into their sexual past. Their bitter-sweet memories form the heart of this book. I hope I have done them justice and that my interpretations are not too far wide of the mark. Many of my contacts came as a result of hundreds of letters published in local and national newspapers. Thank you to all those editors – too numerous to mention – who kindly co-operated with me.

For valuable criticisms and suggestions for changes I am indebted to Paul Thompson of the University of Essex, Nickie Clemens and Gavin Weightman of London Weekend Television, Joanna Mack of Domino Films, Lesley Hall of the Wellcome Institute and Jeff Weeks of the CNAA.

I also owe an enormous debt to many friends and colleagues interested in life stories who I hounded over the months for new information and interviewees. Thanks to Tricia Adams, Rob Wilkinson of the Walthamstow History Group, Karl Major and Rosemary Dixon of the London Sound and Video Archive, Rob Perks of the Bradford Heritage Recording Unit, David Dougan of the Fawcett Library, Peter Everett of BBC Manchester, Annabel Farraday of the Lesbian Archive, John Walton and Bob Poole of the University of Lancaster, Michelle Abenstern, Susan O'Malley of the Open University, John Francombe of Middlesex Polytechnic, Russell Davies of University College Wales, Janet Saunders, formerly of the University of Warwick, Roy Porter of the Wellcome Institute, Brenda Corti and Ken Plummer of the University of Essex, Anna Clarke, Bob Little, The Pennine Heritage Group, Bristol Broadsides, Arthur Wood of Radio Stoke, York Oral History Project, The North West Sound Archive, The Hall-Carpenter Archives, Alan Ward of the National Sound Archive, Maurice Keen of Balliol College, Oxford, Harry Hendrick of Oxford Polytechnic, Phil Cohen of the Institute of Education, University of London, Stephen Dowding, the National Council For One Parent Families, Lynn Jamieson of Edinburgh University, Bill Williams of the Jewish Museum, Manchester, Terry Charman of the Imperial War Museum, Colin Ward, Sheila Jemima of Southampton Record Office, Professor Christopher Smout of St Andrew's University, The Gay Bereavement Group and the Leicester Oral History Project. Special thanks to Doc Rowe of the London Sound and Video

Archive for his help with interviewees, tape recorders and photographs.

Some of the quotations in this book are taken from life story archives. For permission to publish these extracts and for valuable advice, thank you to Paul Thompson (Family Life and Work Experience Archive, University of Essex), Dermot Healey and Audrey Linkman (Manchester Studies Collection, Manchester Polytechnic), Elizabeth Roberts (Centre for North West Regional Studies Collection, University of Lancaster), and to Dorothy Sheridan and her staff at the Mass Observation Archive, University of Sussex. Thanks also to Jonathan Cape for permission to use extracts published in Angus Calder and Dorothy Sheridan, *Speak for Yourself: A Mass Observation Anthology 1937–49* (1984), and to Orbis Books for permission to publish two extracts from Margaret Pringle, *Dance Little Ladies: The Days of the Debutante* (1977).

Many other people have helped in one way or another to make this book possible. Thanks to Barry Cox, Tony Cohen and Pat Newbert for arranging leave from LWT to write it, and to Carey Smith of Sidgwick and Jackson for believing in the project. Thanks again to Sarah Adair, Anne Cornell and Mark Noades for much good humoured help and advice from the LWT Library, and special thanks to Linda Stradling for her unflinching support and her rapid production of a typescript from a set of practically inaudible cassette tapes.

For help with the illustrations in the book thanks to Doc Rowe for his photographs of old newspapers, magazines and archival material; to the Church Army for access to their remarkable archive; to Colindale Newspaper Library; to the ever helpful staff of the London Library; and to Bernard Howarth Loomes, Peter Lawrence, Doug Lear, Billie Love and Lady Marguerite Tangye for help over and above the call of duty in digging out pictures from their extraordinary collections.

Finally, thanks to Peter Salmon and Colin Cameron of the BBC for making the television series based on the book possible. And thanks to Pamela Gordon and Suzanne Power for their tireless work finding interviewees for the television programmes.

INTRODUCTION: TABOO TALK

When the children of the 1960s become grandparents many will perhaps be able to talk to their grandchildren about sex. As a generation they grew up in an era of sexual revolution, when taboos were broken and intimate details of the bedroom were discussed in newspapers, on the radio and on television. But the generations brought up earlier this century, and in fact right up to the early 1950s, did not discuss sex in public. There were very few studies of their sexual behaviour by medical researchers and sociologists. The Victorian legacy was one of public inhibition and silence. This book, and the television series based on it, breaks that silence. Here old-age pensioners talk, sometimes for the first time, about the sexual experiences of their young days. They pull back the covers on a secret world of sex before marriage in the first half of the twentieth century. This book has none of the intricate detail of a modern clinical or psychological examination of sex: that is not the point of it. I am not a sex researcher in the great tradition of Alfred Kinsey or Shire Hite. When I began interviewing I knew my own inhibitions would make me shrink from asking a 92-year-old lady – if I could find one to ask – about her orgasms. What intrigued me much more was the way in which sexual experience or inexperience influenced young people's lives. For young single people who made love before the war did so in a social world which was very different to that of today. There was greater respect or fear of adult authority; the young had fewer rights; the Church had more power over young minds; men and women had much more sharply defined roles; and the workhouse not the welfare state beckoned the young single-parent family. Perhaps most important of all, it seemed that to have sex before marriage was to break a powerful taboo in pre-war Britain.

I began my research in 1981 by putting a letter, asking for memories of young love and sexual experience, in practically every local newspaper in Britain. I rather pompously signed myself as Dr Humphries and gave the address as the University of Essex – where I was then a lecturer – in order to try to reassure people that this was an academically respectable request for information. For to be honest, if I was an elderly person living alone I would be very wary of answering a letter of this sort, and even more wary of inviting a stranger into my home to discuss my sex life. Over the next few months I received around 200 replies; some of them were rapidly written notes, penned, so they said, when nobody was in the house, others major epics which must have taken many hours to compose. I even got one extraordinary letter from a former proprietor of a surgical supply stores in Chesterfield who had been imprisoned for two years for performing an illegal abortion. A few people scribbled messages on the envelopes – probably done at the last moment before posting – which showed they were worried they had given too much away. One read, 'Please don't send anything through post that my husband could use against me. Life is too short. Thank you.' Some agreed to be interviewed, but a number of these letter-writers felt they couldn't talk face to face, preferring instead a clandestine correspondence. By now the embarrassment and sometimes the hurt of my correspondents was beginning to get to me and I agonized as to whether I was rather mischievously stirring up feelings that were best left alone. My worries were heightened by the fact that a few women who wrote to me assumed I was a doctor of medicine – which I am not – and told me about their sex lives in the hope that I would give them medical advice for various problems. Then Radio One and the popular dailies ran the story that a sex-mad doctor was doing some digging into grannies' private lives and I was dubbed by one 'the dirty doctor'. I began to get a trickle of hate mail. My colleagues, who had always seen this as a rather dubious piece of research anyway, began to snigger and wink. At this point – rather feebly in retrospect – I gave up.

Five years later I decided to pick up the threads of the research again. One day whilst flicking through the box files of extraordinary letters that I had received, it struck me forcibly that some, perhaps nearly all of these people were now dead. Many had been well into their seventies when they had originally written to me, and others were past ninety. If their stories were to be recorded it would have to be done now. I wrote to some of my most outstanding respondents and found my gloomy fears were well-founded: half of the letters were returned by the Post Office or by new residents with the information that they were not known at that address or were dead. Eventually I managed to contact and persuade about twenty of my original respondents to talk to me, one or two of them still going strong in their mid-nineties.

But this hardly seemed a large enough sample to say a great deal about. I needed more people to talk to and tried to get them through a variety of means. I had left university to enter the world of television making social history programmes and over the years I had built up a large contact book of interviewees, all of whom had excellent recall of their young days. Several agreed to talk to me about sex before marriage. Also I went prospecting amongst many friends involved in oral history projects all over Britain and occasionally struck gold with some likely names they gave me. By the spring of 1986 I had managed to assemble a grand total of about sixty interviewees who were prepared to talk to me. My main criterion for selection was experience of sex before marriage, a vivid memory of the experience and a willingness to talk openly and honestly about it. I gave myself six months to do the interviews.

As the day approached when I was to do my first interview I began to

understand why so few people had done this sort of thing before. The taboo on talking about sex to someone born as long ago as the Edwardian era has a powerful resonance which is very difficult to duck. Few of us can imagine ringing up our granny or an aged aunt, or perhaps even less our parents, to arrange to speak to them about the secret sex life of their youth. This, in a sense, was what I had chosen to spend six months doing, though it was somebody else's granny, aunt or parents I was talking to. Even at this early stage I was sure that if I had been related or too close to these people they would not have talked to me openly, if at all, for fear of 'shameful' stories getting out in the family. Some had already told me that they had never spoken before about lots of the sexual escapades of their youth, sometimes not even to their husband or wife, and they were still anxious to keep these secrets from them. Where their stories appear in the book I have used pseudonyms for obvious reasons.

I arranged my first interview with Ted Harrison, a jovial, warm-hearted Londoner, a retired electrician, now in his late eighties. He lives in a dingy but very homely council flat in Hoxton, North London, an area where he has spent the whole of his life. Since I first met him five years ago when looking for first-hand accounts of slum life in the capital before the First World War, Ted has never ceased to amaze me with his sharp and amusing stories. He has a remarkable recall of the distant past. You feel you could talk to Ted about anything and learn something new. He seemed the best person to start with. I typed up a fifteen-page questionnaire which I intended to plough through during the interview. But almost as soon as I had finished it I realized I would never use it, at least not in this or any other interview itself. It seemed insulting and insensitive to be brandishing a set of bureaucratic-looking papers when talking about so personal and sensitive a subject. It might well have created an unnecessarily formal atmosphere and killed my rapport stone-dead. I decided that I would start with some talk about childhood, work and courtship, then gradually ease the conversation around to sex, letting the interviewee take me wherever he or she wanted, though to be honest I did have certain key questions that I was fairly determined to ask, come what may. This formula seemed to work well with Ted and I used it in most of my subsequent interviews. Ted, it turned out, had learned what little he knew about the facts of life from older boys and girls on the streets of the capital. He fell in love with his wife-to-be Jenny, an operative at the local boot and shoe factory, when he was seventeen. While courting they used to make love late at night on top of a coster's barrow parked near the street where he lived. Ted and Jenny knew nothing about contraception and she quickly became pregnant. They hurriedly married to avoid bringing shame on their families.

My first interview proved to me that it was possible to break down the taboos which normally block conversations about sex with people of this generation. I spent the next three months dashing madly around

Britain with a tape recorder and a big bag of tapes, going from one interview to the next. In a sense it seemed like a race against time or – without being too melodramatic – against death. Many of my interviewees were very old and frail, a few had terminal illnesses and I was frightened that some would die before I could record their story. It was a possibility that they were very aware of, but luckily all lived to speak to me.

The interviews themselves were the most moving I have ever done. They often started awkwardly: there would be an atmosphere of tension and embarrassment, spiked with difficult silences. But after fifteen or twenty minutes the talk would generally flow much more freely. Long ago hurts would come back, lost loves were remembered, the joys and injustices of the past were relived, often with laughter, less often with tears. Sometimes we would both get so engrossed in a conversation that we forgot to eat or drink for three or four hours. The overwhelming emotion which was conveyed, however, was one of pain, suggesting a violence that was done to young minds and bodies. This was especially true of women who – as always in my experience – express their emotions much more easily than men. Perhaps surprising was the fact that my being a man didn't seem to make any difference to what they told me about their sex lives.

The hardback edition of this book, first published in the summer of 1988, attracted enormous publicity which encouraged me to approach the BBC with the idea of a television series based on it. However, turning the book into television programmes proved far more difficult than I first imagined. Sadly, a few of my original interviewees had by now died and a number of others were unwilling to face the glare of publicity that appearing on television would inevitably involve. Sex talk is still very much forbidden territory amongst the over sixties and even today few are prepared publicly to break this taboo. Consequently we had to undertake a new research project to find more people who were willing to speak on television, which again involved hundreds of letters to newspapers and visits to old people's homes. As a result some of those who appear in the book are not in the television series and vice versa.

Though the interviews – both for the book and for the television series – were deeply moving, I sometimes felt, as American oral historian Studs Terkel once put it, like 'a thief in the night'. You go in, you search for the most private and intimate story of a person's life, then you rush off to the next interview where the same thing happens again. The ritual cup of tea after the interview, the handshake and peck on the cheek, and the letter of thanks do little to allay this uncomfortable feeling. The justification, I suppose, is that this was the only way the book and the television series based on it could have been completed.

FORBIDDEN FRUIT

Ada Haskins, the daughter of a miner, was born in 1911 in the tiny mining village of Winlaton, County Durham. At the age of sixteen she was sent to London to enter service. Most of her first two years in service were spent paying back her coach fare to the capital and the cost of her uniform. But in 1930 she went home for a long working holiday to help her mother look after her new baby sister. The holiday was to change her life in a most tragic way. She became pregnant the first time she ever made love with a man – a young sailor from a neighbouring village whom she'd been going out with for several months. A marriage was quickly arranged by the parents for the teenage couple but she was jilted on the morning of the wedding when the groom fled to sea to avoid his responsibilities. Ada's mother was deeply ashamed of her pregnant daughter and three months later she turned her out of the family home and sent her to a workhouse at nearby Chester-le-Street to have the baby:

> When my labour started, I'll never forget that morning; I couldn't believe that pain could be so atrocious. I just stood there with my hands on the table and this matron came back and she said, 'What's the matter with you? Get on with your work!' 'Oh,' I said, 'I can't, I've got the most terrible pain.' She said, 'That'll go away, then it'll come back again, then it'll go away and it'll come back again. Now carry on.' So in between I'm trying to scrub. 'Oh, dear God,' I thought, 'this can't go on for much longer.' And all of a sudden the waters broke, all the floor was wet. 'Course, that was it. They called me everything for wetting the floor. They got me up to the Labour Ward, but after that I went through hell. . . . I screamed my lungs out with pain, and one matron came in and said, 'Concentrate on what you're doing. You knew what you were doing when you got yourself into this state, now you've got to get yourself out of it!' Afterwards they said, 'Oh, she'll need about eight stitches now,' and nothing, no chloroform, eight stitches, I mean it was dreadful. And the doctor says, 'You've got a boy, seven pounds, four ounces.' When I said, 'Call me Ada, that's my name,' they didn't want to know. No, you weren't a human being.

Ada Haskins, aged nineteen, in 1930. Several months after this picture was taken, she was in the workhouse with an illegitimate baby

The baby was brought up by Ada's mother who pretended – as did the whole of the family – that it was hers. Ada returned to work in service in London and sent ten shillings a week out of her wages of ten and sixpence to feed and clothe her son. She continued to provide for him until he was fourteen and came back home to see him whenever she could, usually twice a year. She too kept the secret, and her son always knew her as his sister. Now Ada wants to tell the truth to her son, but fears she never will:

> I send him five pounds for his birthday present and he returns it to me with a note saying, 'Spend it on yourself, Sis, you can't afford it,' and it upsets me quite a bit. I've been up there three or four times to try and tell him before I die that I'm his mother but I just can't go through with it. He's fifty-seven now himself and it would be such a shock for him I don't know if he could accept it. Sometimes I think it's God punishing me for the sin of having an illegitimate child. I married afterwards, a very happy marriage and we desperately wanted children but couldn't have any. My only son doesn't know I'm his mother.

Ada Haskins' story gives us a glimpse into a secret world of sex in Britain during the first half of our century. She broke two powerful sexual taboos of her time: the taboo which forbade sexual experience to young people outside marriage, and the taboo of bearing a bastard child. Sadly – and unfairly – she has carried the shame and stigma of this through the rest of her life. This kind of forbidden fruit of the past forms the core of this book. It is based on stories of secret sex of young lovers between the 1900s and the 1950s. Many still cannot or will not speak honestly of the sexual experiences they may have had in their young days. But the more liberal atmosphere which has surrounded sexuality in the last thirty years, has encouraged a few older people to talk more openly. By listening to their memories we can gain a unique insight into an important area of human experience about which we know almost nothing. Their life stories bring to light a forgotten yet controversial chapter in British social history.

Most of us born in the post-war years have some sort of mental snapshot – or a series of snapshots – of the look and life style of young lovers before the last war. The twenties' image is of 'let's do it' bright young things, dancing the Charleston, mad cocktail parties, fast cars, and liberated young women with short hair and short skirts, shocking their elders. The thirties' image is softer and more romantic: smoochy nightclubs and sophisticated women emulating the latest feminine fashions from Hollywood. Most of these images are drawn from old movies, newsreels and popular accounts of the period, and in some ways they reflect real social changes after the First World War. Many young men and even more young women had a new look in the inter-war years which was often smart and distinctively modern. Increasing affluence, especially in the booming south-east, and the emerging fashion industries which produced cheap clothes and cosmetics for a mass market meant that away from work it was becoming increasingly difficult to tell people's class by the way they dressed. J. B. Priestley on his *English Journey* in the 1930s noted that 'factory girls

On holiday on the Isle of Thanet, 1929. The cigarette-smoking girl of the period created an illusion of sexual sophistication

looking like actresses' was one of the new features of the modern world.

It is only when you begin to talk seriously to people about the lives and loves of their young days that you start to realize how little these images correspond to what they were really doing and thinking. These images are heavily stylized and glamorized, some of them coming from Hollywood's dream machine. And they are often set in the exclusive world of the rich and famous. They are particularly misleading if the assumption is made – as it was both at the time and still is today – that this much more self-consciously sexual appearance was somehow a reflection of much greater sexual awareness and freedom. They make the pre-war years seem tantalizingly close when in fact a deep gulf separates us. The cigarette-smoking girl of the period with her bright lipstick and rouge created an illusion of sexual sophistication. Beneath this mask lay enormous pressures for sexual conformity.

The taboo on sex before marriage which was in part the legacy of the Victorian age remained immensely powerful right up until the 1950s –

and arguably beyond. What is most striking, looking back especially to Edwardian and inter-war Britain, is that all the institutions that really mattered when it came to moulding the minds of young people and supervising them on a day-to-day basis, took a hard line on what was called 'promiscuity'. Only those who came from either very rich or very poor backgrounds – as we will see later – managed to escape this control. Parents issued dire warnings against sex before marriage especially to daughters, and as far as they could, controlled the sexual behaviour of their children to make sure they didn't step out of line. Most schools, training colleges and youth organizations were sex

A popular magazine for young women in the 1930s. Journals like this promoted romance and femininity, but sex outside marriage remained taboo

segregated and tried to limit and control the contact between members of the opposite sex. Churches – which wielded much greater power before the last war – continued to preach the gospel of the sanctity of marriage and the sin of 'fornication'. Sexual respectability was considered very important in many office jobs like banking and insurance, and if there was evidence of sexual misconduct a young man or woman's career prospects could be ruined. The police or vigilante patrols warned or arrested young people who became too amorous in public places. Social workers had the power to place 'promiscuous' girls in institutional care. Young women who had children outside marriage had very few rights and were often humiliated and sadistically treated in workhouses, infirmaries and Mother-and-Baby homes. The new BBC under Lord Reith would not broadcast anything in the way of comedy, drama, talks or music which had a whiff of sexual unconventionality about it. Lord Reith would not even allow anyone who was a divorcee to work at the BBC. Rigorous censorship ensured that no films showing 'promiscuous' scenes were screened in cinemas. The legendary cinematic convention for bedroom scenes was 'one foot on the floor at all times'. Sex education books, without exception, prescribed abstinence and chastity for the unmarried. Chemists often refused to sell contraceptives to single people. Even sex reformers like Marie Stopes, the pioneer of birth-control clinics in the inter-war years, found 'promiscuity' distasteful and immoral. Her clinics only provided advice and contraception for married couples. While there was some relaxation of the old puritanical attitudes towards sex in marriage there was little or no easing up in the sexual restraint expected of young people.

Sex before marriage was attacked so strongly – and sometimes hysterically – for a number of reasons. The concern with the moral control of young people was of paramount importance and this control was frequently used for religious, political or ideological motives. But it is important not to forget some of the practical dangers of sex in the first half of our century. Contraception was far less safe than it is today. In the 1930s it was commonly believed that almost half of all condoms on the market were faulty in some way. There was also a series of epidemics of venereal disease, the most serious one being around the time of the First World War. According to the Royal Commission on the disease in 1916 10 per cent of the male population had syphilis and far more gonorrhoea. There was at this time no cure for syphilis and gonorrhoea was difficult and painful to treat. The atmosphere of fear which venereal disease created – often whipped up by moral reform groups – was similar to that today over AIDS.

The most influential group of people, who more than any other preached sexual restraint and promoted Victorian attitudes towards the sex life of young people well into the twentieth century, were those who made up what was called the 'Social Purity and Hygiene Movement'. This was a pressure-group drawn from all walks of life, especially from

the ranks of the church and the medical and teaching professions, but with strong backing amongst all political parties – the Labour prime minister Ramsay MacDonald was an ardent supporter. The movement began in the late nineteenth century as a crusade against the evils of prostitution and pornography which were seen to be increasing and were – it was claimed – threatening the moral fibre of the nation. Early feminists were in the forefront of this crusade and they waged a courageous battle against the double standard of sexual morality which turned a blind eye to all sorts of sexual indulgences for men, but expected women to remain chaste and submissive. By the early 1900s the movement became increasingly concerned with the problem of promiscuity and the sexual morals of young people. It had helped to raise the age of consent from thirteen to sixteen in 1885, partly to protect young girls from prostitution. Now it declared war on masturbation, then around the time of the First World War, it switched its attention to the problem of venereal disease, advocating chastity – especially amongst the young – as the only way of avoiding its spread. During the First World War it also responded to the panic about promiscuity by helping to organize night-time patrols of middle-class

A Church Army caravan 'on the road' around the turn of the century. The Church Army were strong supporters of the Social Purity and Hygiene Movement which advocated chastity among young people

Social Purity reformers found this kind of Edwardian postcard, typical of the period, deeply offensive. The wearing of body stockings (to mask the 'naughty bits') in some ways heightens its sexuality

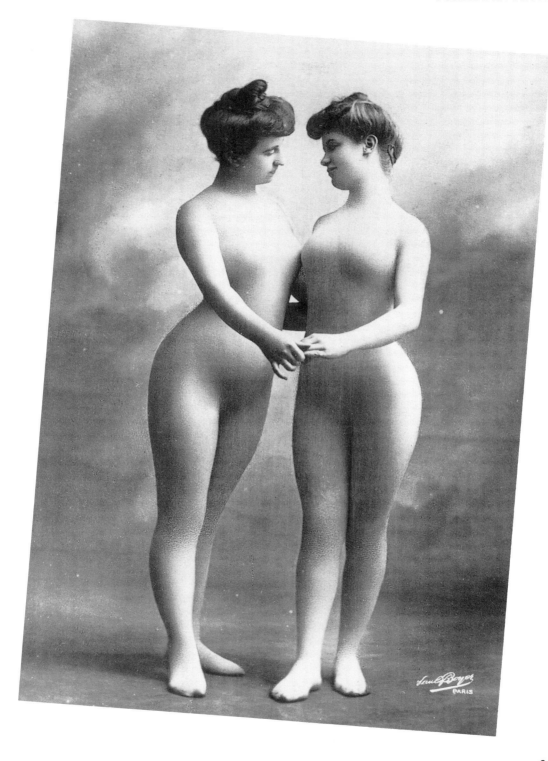

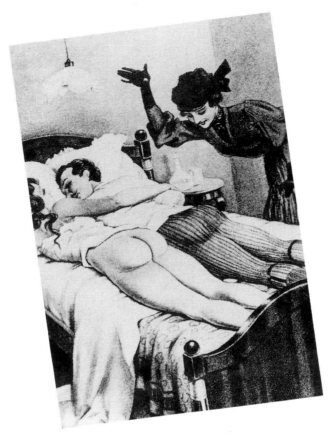

Edwardian 'spanking' postcard.
By the standards of the time, this
was shocking and pornographic

ladies to stop immoral behaviour in parks and around the military
camps which had sprouted up all over Britain. These vigilante groups,
known as Voluntary Women's Patrols, scoured places like Hampstead
Heath and Hyde Park in London, accosting amorous couples and
reporting their offences to parents and the police. One consequence of
this zeal was the entry of women into the police force – by 1918 these
patrols had become professionalized and were part of the Metropolitan
Police Force. By this time the religious element in the movement was
being overshadowed by a 'scientific', eugenist concern with the
strength and purity of the British race. The emphasis on the importance of chastity for the young, however, remained much the same. The
Social Purity and Hygiene Movement remained influential during the
inter-war years, dominating sex education in schools and encouraging
controls on censorship and obscenity, especially in the cinema which
was so popular with young people. And although most of these pressure
groups disappeared after the Second World War their ideals remained
at the heart of 'public morality' in Britain until the mid-1950s.

Many of the books, articles, pamphlets and newspapers produced by
the Social Purity and Hygiene Movement are lovingly preserved in the

Fawcett Library in London and in the archives of the Church Army and the Salvation Army. Looking through their pages you enter a lost world of moral certainty, sexual prudery and Christian zeal. The unashamed desire for a racially 'pure' stock and the faith in science to achieve this by interfering in people's sex lives were also very important. The titles of the movement's newspapers, like *The Shield*, *Prevention*, *Seeking and Saving*, *Deliverer*, *Chivalry*, *On Guard*, and *The Vigilance Record*, conjure up this militant and evangelical attitude towards the prevention of sex. Reformers were in part trying to protect young women from the attentions of predatory men. The unscrupulous and sometimes violent behaviour of some men recorded in this book suggests that there was a big need for a movement in defence of women. However, the campaigners often did more harm than good, inadvertently contributing to the unhappiness and social ruin of some of the young women they claimed to be helping. For although they sympathized with the innocent girl who was seduced, they were often very hostile towards the 'unashamed' promiscuous young woman who indulged in sex outside marriage. She was blamed for spreading venereal disease. And in so doing she was thought to be putting the very future of the British race at risk. These young women were referred to in the social purity literature as 'amateurs', meaning amateur prostitutes. Some investigators and writers clearly found it almost unimaginable that a woman would consent to 'casual sex' unless she was a prostitute. And the 'amateur' was thought to be a major social problem. The image they created was of a growing army of young women from all social classes who openly defied sexual convention and were happy to agree to casual sex, preferably in return for some gift or favour. They explained the decline in professional prostitution during the 1920s and 1930s in terms of the increase in the numbers of these 'promiscuous amateurs'. As Gladys Hall put it in *Prostitution: A Survey and a Challenge* in 1933:

> The chief explanation of the decreased demand for professional prostitutes is the intrusion into the prostitute's sphere of the amateur, or, as the professional describes her, 'the straight girl'. In other words, a man may, at the present time, have opportunities for promiscuous sex relations with girls from among his own social group whom he knows, or whose acquaintance he may readily make; and there are methods whereby in the course of conversation, this fact is conveyed to him. Although he usually pays for his satisfaction, the payment takes the form of a gift, or a dinner, or a motor run; the episode appears less commercial and suggests more of a passion and spontaneity than a similar episode with a professional prostitute, and for this reason is usually infinitely more attractive. . . . 'I hadn't walked out with her properly more than once,' was the remark of a town youth to a woman patrol, going on to explain that by 'walking out properly' he meant having sexual intercourse during the walk.

A policewoman chases naked young bathers away from the Serpentine in Hyde Park, London, in 1926. One of the main duties of early policewomen was to prevent 'immoral behaviour' in parks and other public places

There are many Social Purity and Hygiene books and reports containing evidence like this – but their inbuilt bias presents a serious problem. This is where living memory becomes very important, for it has a different and much more authentic story to tell. It provides an alternative view of events from the point of view of the people – especially the women – who are being sanctimoniously criticized or attacked in these accounts. I have spoken to or corresponded with many women who experienced sex before marriage during the inter-war years and their approach to sex bears little or no resemblance to the stereotype of the 'amateur'. Most tasted the 'forbidden fruit' either because they felt a strong attraction or affection for somebody, or because they were 'in love'.

Often the man put pressure on the woman to consummate the relationship before marriage, though if she 'gave in' too easily he might cynically reject her in favour of another and sometimes young women were forced to have sex against their will. All this suggests that sex was far from casual for single women. Most would only entertain sex within a serious relationship or courtship. And most were terrified of being caught – a fear that led many couples into a constant search for safe places to make love. As a teenager in the early 1930s Mary Young worked at the Wills's Tobacco Factory in Bedminster, Bristol. There is little doubt that she would have been described in the Social Purity literature of the day as an 'amateur' and had her case been reported she may even have been placed in institutional care by moral welfare workers. This is the way she sees it:

> When I was a young girl from fourteen to eighteen I was never allowed to have a boyfriend and was allowed two nights a week out. I had to be home by nine in the evenings sharp or else. I had a few casual boyfriends when I was eighteen but Mother always terminated them. She was very strict and very Edwardian in her ways and ideas. I abided by them and never dared to answer back or defy. But between the ages of eighteen and nineteen I became rather fond of my girlfriend's brother. We met secretly on my nights out and eventually love blossomed. But unfortunately a neighbour saw us together and told my mother. I received a severe thrashing with a cane and was stopped from having my two nights out for two weeks and told what would happen if I didn't give up my boy. I was most unhappy so needless to say I continued to see him. There were continual rows with Mother and one night she beat me so severely I had to stay home from work until the marks healed up. Mother insisted he was a waster. . . . We went steady for some time before anything like sex was even mentioned. Then one summer evening we were strolling through some fields and decided to sit down. We kissed passionately and spoke of our love for each other. After a while he undid the fastenings on my blouse, slipped his hand inside and began to fondle my breast,

Fairground scene at Southend-on-Sea, Essex, in the 1930s

whilst his other hand entered my lower undergarments and he proceeded to fondle my private parts. This continued for a while – still kissing passionately – when I realized he was much aroused. So, too, was I and he rolled over on to me. It was my first experience of sex although he withdrew just before the climax. I found I quite enjoyed it and from that time on it happened many times between us. Even in a picture house we would touch each other and often on our way home would stop in some dark secluded place and satisfy our desires. . . . Every time we went walking on summer evenings we always took to the fields, wading through long mowing grass to Long Ashton until we found a space far away from passers-by or prying eyes. There we laid down and made love. I can't really say which of us was the keenest. I think we were equal.

It was a feeling we couldn't control once we were close to each other. In the winter when it was cold and windy we would stand by a sheltered stile, just off the main Bridgwater Road. One night a terrific thunder storm occurred. There was nowhere to shelter except for an old farm cart standing there so we crept underneath that and waited for the storm to abate. The next morning before leaving for work I noticed large patches of black oil all over the back of my coat. I was scared stiff and knew I had to get rid of the oil marks before Mother discovered it. I walked to work with one thought in my mind, how to get rid of the oil marks. I was so worried that I told a friend at work about it. She took me to her house after we left work and between us we rubbed away at the oil marks with paraffin. Sure enough it worked but the smell of paraffin lingered so my friend poured her perfume over my coat. One day just after this Mother said there was a smell of paraffin in the hall where my coat hung. I was so petrified with fear of her finding out – she would have skinned me alive – but thankfully nothing came of it. Another time was when my boy and I were lying under a huge oak tree down in what we called the pitfields. We had our usual session until suddenly we heard a noise like a branch breaking. We looked up and there from the branches was a face peeking down at us. It was a man, well known as 'Dogger Davies'. There were several of that sort living on Bedminster Down in those days. He approached us and I realized he was my brother's father-in-law. He said he had watched everything and was going to tell my parents unless we paid him money. My boy was unemployed and I had very little pocket money on me, but between us we scraped together half a crown which we gave to Dogger, who promised to say nothing about the incident.

Here we have the authentic voice of a young woman in love. This kind of first-hand testimony strips away the layers of prejudice that moral crusaders often grafted on to 'promiscuity'. Just as life stories can tell us much about the social and psychological side of sex before marriage, so can they tell us something about the physical side of relationships. Through people's stories we can discover much about the nitty gritty of illicit sex in the past which moral reformers knew little or nothing of or were too prudish to record. It seems likely, according to many people, that the most common form of intercourse indulged in by young people was sex standing up – known colloquially as the 'knee trembler'. Sex standing up seems to have been most prevalent in working-class areas of towns and cities and was usually indulged in against walls and dark alleys in the evening. Those who had a park or secluded open space near to hand and those who lived in the suburbs close to the countryside obviously enjoyed more opportunities. But for most city youths there was simply no other way or place to do it. It was a form of sex that was fast, furtive and rarely fulfilling for young women. Bill Phillips remembers this kind of illicit street sex from his courting days in the East End of London during the 1920s:

Saying goodnight after an evening at the pictures. Very often sexual intercourse among young working-class couples took place standing up in dark alleys

They called it knee tremblers; when you were near enough coming to a climax your knees did tremble. You'd get in a doorway with a girl and there'd be a stand-up sex sort of thing. Mind you, it'd be a struggle because sometimes the girl was bigger than you and sometimes she was smaller. Sometimes you had to half bend and sometimes you'd have to get her to come down towards you. And of course it was a strain really. Then all of a sudden your knees would start to tremble. Then you'd say 'done it', so it was like that. When you were in your prime really and you hadn't had a bit for say two or three days, you would be about ten minutes I suppose. You'd take them round the docklands, round the warehouses in wide doorways, wherever you could where there wasn't houses nearby. And you would have stand up ones in the doorway. . . . I was in a doorway once and a policewoman came past, well we looked out for them, and I saw her coming and we had to run. Mind you if they caught you, they took you to the police station and they would class her as a prostitute, though she wasn't a prostitute. They would class her as a prostitute if she was caught having sex in the street. Then once they were branded prostitutes they'd always be a prostitute.

In rural areas young village couples would, in fine weather during the spring and summer, find secluded spots in which to lie down, but for the rest of the year stand-up sex was as common as it was in the cities. Jack Baker, a young footman in the 1920s, recalls the goings-on in the lanes and fields around the Dorset country estate where he worked:

It was the usual thing in those days as I was motorcycling along the country roads, nearly every farm gate would be occupied by a courting couple on certain nights of the week, Friday night, Saturday night, pay night and sometimes Sunday. And that was the main place where courting took place. Quite often it was quite plain to see they were having sex, people used to pass by and nothing was said or taken any notice of whatsoever. Of course the position they had was that they were standing up most of the time. And that was one of my regular positions for sex, standing up, especially in the winter when it was impossible to lie in the fields. You'd stand against the gate or in some secluded spot. It was less satisfying. It was a well-known thing, and the term that the boys had for it was a knee trembler.

So far I have highlighted some of the advantages of life stories as a way of getting into this forbidden territory. Yet there can be problems: memory and experience are as subject to distortion as any other form of historical evidence whether it be government statistics, press reports, social investigations, autobiography or whatever. Sometimes the bias is of a conscious nature, sometimes it is unconscious and unintended. And although older people's long-term memory is often quite accurate they can forget, invent and exaggerate what really happened. The individuals quoted in this book are involved in as much of a reconstruction of the past as this book is in trying to make sense of their collective experience. I have tried to ensure that the testimony I have used is authentic by looking for internal consistency in the evidence and crosschecking information where possible. But it might be argued that personal accounts of sexual experience are one of the most unreliable forms of evidence. Stories of sexual exploits are the stuff of which gossip is made and many of us have probably dressed up our sexual experiences to impress or to be entertaining. Some recent research has shown that young people are one of the most likely groups of all to be dishonest about their experience of sex – or lack of it. Crude sexism seems to play a large part in this. Boys tend to exaggerate their 'conquests' to appear 'manly', while girls usually play down sexual experience for the sake of respectability and to avoid a reputation as a 'slag'.

It seems to me, in answer to this kind of criticism, that old people are not under the same pressure to make wild or false claims about the sexual experiences of their youth. In a serious one-to-one interview which goes into the intimate details of affairs and courtships with lovers, wives or husbands who are now often dead, it seems there is in fact a reverse pressure – to discover the truth and significance of it all. I was constantly moved by the care that many interviewees took to be accurate, to avoid bias and to try to come to a dispassionate understanding of their past relationships. Where sexual experience led, as was not infrequently the case, to some kind of family drama or personal tragedy, many people were surprised at what an emotional release it was to tell their story honestly after many years of secrecy and repression. Some found tears streaming down their faces when talking about events that happened more than fifty years ago. This cathartic side of the interviews must provide some measure of the authenticity of the experience that is being recalled.

Another problem with the life stories I have collected touches on how far they can be seen to be representative of more general trends in sexual experience during the first half of our century. Since sexuality is still very much a taboo subject amongst older people I have found it impossible to question the kind of representative sample that is normally sought in social surveys. Even though I tried to draw my interviewees from all social classes and all parts of Britain, they, in a sense, selected themselves by choosing to talk about their sex lives. This makes them an unusual group of people in the first place. As long as talking about sex remains taboo amongst large numbers of people this will always remain a serious problem in this kind of research.

But to try to put the life stories told by my interviewees into a broader perspective and to avoid too many distortions when generalizing from personal experiences into social trends, I have drawn on the findings of the handful of British sex surveys completed in the late 1940s and early

1950s. Most of them were largely based on the anonymous filling in of questionnaires sent through the post. The largest was Eustace Chesser's survey of the sex lives of over 6,000 women published as *The Sexual, Marital and Family Relationships of the English Woman*, in 1956. There was the study, 'General Attitudes to Sex' – which questioned several hundred men and women – completed in 1949 by Tom Harrisson's remarkable research organization, Mass Observation. There was Eliot Slater and Moya Woodside's sex survey of 200 working-class couples in London during the 1940s and published in 1951 as *Patterns of Marriage*. And there was Geoffrey Gorer's *Exploring English Character* published in 1955 which contained a survey of sexual attitudes based on the responses of 5,000 readers of *The People* newspaper. These surveys, the first to really break the taboo on asking any questions about sex in Britain, contain fascinating information on sex during the early part of the century when some of the respondents were young. They provide some evidence that there was a gradual increase in the frequency of sex before marriage over the decades, indicating a growing relaxation of Victorian taboos between the 1900s and the 1950s. Eustace Chesser, for example, found that 19 per cent of married women born before 1904 had pre-marital sex; this rose to 36 per cent for those born between 1904 and 1914; it rose again to 39 per cent for those born between 1914 and 1924; and it finally rose to 43 per cent for those born between 1924 and 1934. There are, it must be said, many problems in the sampling and accuracy of these surveys. They, too, found it difficult or impossible to find representative samples; the surveys of both Chesser and Mass Observation were slightly weighted

Theatrical postcard for *Oh I Say* – one of the many productions looking at the lives and loves of the 'new woman' during the early part of the century

This saucy postcard was sent to a Miss Jessie Jones in North Wales in 1906. The message on the back reads 'Who's the guilty one? E.'

"STOP YER TICKLING, JOCK!"

in favour of middle-class respondents, usually of a liberal turn of mind. And the Slater and Woodside survey, though it contains interesting information on sexuality, was primarily a study of neurosis; as a consequence half the male respondents were soldiers who had been hospitalized for neurotic and other illnesses during the Second World War. In addition there was always some suspicion – given the fact that there was still a stigma about sex before marriage – whether inter- viewees were telling the truth. Slater and Woodside, for example, were fairly certain that some of their interviewees were covering up pre- marital sex out of embarrassment. Although only 58 per cent of men and 34 per cent of women told them they had had sex before marriage, they thought the true figures were closer to 75 per cent for men and 50 per cent for women. The questionnaires used in many of these surveys often tended to encourage a fairly narrow range of response, and they never focused primarily on sex before marriage. But despite drawbacks like these the surveys did at least question a large number of people about sex in the first half of our century, many of whom were middle aged and whose youthful experiences were still fresh in their memory. They suggest that by the early 1950s the numbers of people prepared to admit to pre-marital sex had gradually risen to around a half to two-thirds of all married men and a third to a half of all married women. Sex is obviously not a subject which lends itself to accurate statistical analysis and we should allow a large margin for error here. But this is a useful though crude guide to the kind of proportion of the British population that might have tasted the forbidden fruit of sex before marriage in the past.

2

THE FACTS OF LIFE

Bert Mullen was born in 1921, the only son of an engineer, and was brought up on a new inter-war council estate in Fishponds, Bristol. His sexual education began around the age of thirteen:

> We used to spy through a hedge on this couple who went over the Recreation ground and did it. Well, you had to learn something by looking at something like that. Then we used to go out in the country and spot courting couples and see what they were getting up to. Sometimes the bloke would come over shaking his fist, 'Clear off you little swines!' We were only trying to learn something, weren't we? But you couldn't learn much because they all had their clobber on; they were muffed up to the eyeballs. We used to pick up a lot from the older boys. Once I was in chapel and a boy showed us all a contraceptive in a tin. He said he was using it on his girlfriend and was very proud of himself. Then there was this local girl; she used to take us out in the fields away from all the houses and display her wares to us. She'd take her clothes off and sort of put on a show. She was very proud of her body and we thought she was being very kind to let us look and have a feel. Because to us it was the eighth wonder of the world.

This was a fairly typical initiation into the secrets of the world of sex for a boy from a working-class background before the Second World War. Most working-class boys learned what they knew about sex from raw experience on the streets. Although their experiences were a bit crude they often ended up knowing more about sex, at a more tender age, than those from a more well-to-do background. Sexual knowledge certainly had nothing to do with privilege or education. Young people, from whatever background, generally taught each other about the facts of life – though there were strenuous efforts by adults to control their knowledge and keep them in ignorance. This chapter tells the story of what they knew and what they didn't, and how they found out.

Moral reformers constantly complained that poor children knew far too much for their own good. Better-off parents usually exerted greater control over their children's sexual knowledge and development. If a boy or – even more worrying – a girl from a well-to-do background indulged in this kind of sexual experimentation, the parents would usually intervene very rapidly to put an end to it. Lady Marguerite Tangye – née Bligh – remembers her short-lived horseplay with the village boys in Worlingham, Suffolk, during the 1920s:

I used to play with the cook's son who was called Eddie and he and I used to bicycle around the place and play on the roof; he was a great companion. And one day my mother came round the corner of the shrubbery and saw Eddie, who'd just tackled me, playing rugby, lying on top of me and she said, 'You mustn't let the cook's son lie on top of you like that.' And I think at that moment she thought it was time at thirteen that I was sent to school. I'd never been to school up to that time, so I went to a girls' school.

Lady Marguerite Tangye, plus friends, pictured in the early 1920s on the family estate at Worlingham, Suffolk. At the age of thirteen she was packed off to a girls' boarding school, for her family feared she was becoming too familiar with the local boys

Most children of whatever class living in rural areas often enjoyed more freedom than Lady Marguerite. Many took advantage of the opportunities provided by the secluded fields and woods to explore their own bodies and those of the opposite sex. This sexual play was partly inspired, according to some interviewees, by observations of the animals around them. Sometimes these games – often initiated by older girls with boys who were not yet sexually mature – were direct simulations of the sex act. Bill Griffiths, the son of a civil servant, was brought up in a north Cumbrian village during the 1920s:

Living in the country as we did, boys and girls aged, I suppose, in the eight to ten region, saw what farm animals did, and as a result tried to emulate them. Certainly in our village once they knew what to do, the girls made the approach. Barns and stables in unused farm buildings were favourite spots, preferably with lofts containing hay. The girls made the suggestion of what we would play, retire to the loft, remove their knickers and lay on their backs with their legs open and shout 'ready'. One girl in particular would open herself with both hands and made sure you got inside before letting them close on you. I was not too bothered personally and was content to just lay on top but the girls would say, 'Come on, put it in properly' and that was that. There was no pushing in and out as in normal intercourse. It is surprising that we were never caught – and just as well. One girl, a farmer's daughter and somewhat older than the rest, maybe twelve, called it 'bulling', and would invite me to 'bull her'. We once did it spontaneously in the dried up bed of a stream while having a walk in the field.

We tend to make so many assumptions about the total sexual ignorance of children and young people brought up with Victorian sexual conventions, it is perhaps surprising to find that sexual exploration seems to have featured so prominently in their play. They were of course ignorant in many ways about the changes happening to their bodies, and about the mysteries of contraception and child birth. Yet for many it was a strange mixture of innocence and experience. A girl with no knowledge of how a baby was made may have explored the genitals of young boys at street corners and played at 'lovemaking' in the fields. And masturbation, sometimes in groups or gangs, was very common amongst boys as soon as they reached sexual maturity – usually in their early teens. This sexual experimentation was often a cause of great anxiety to adults. This anxiety encouraged parents to issue dire warnings to their children and it helped to fuel campaigns to provide an adult-controlled sex education for young people. In a society in which discipline of the young was a cherished goal amongst all classes, this sexual independence was widely seen to be very dangerous. This fear, as we shall see, helped to shape a very repressive approach to the sexuality of children and young people from late Victorian times onwards.

Sexual play formed part of a primitive culture of the young passed down through word of mouth by generations of schoolboys and schoolgirls. It was intricately bound up with all the strange initiation rites, seasonal customs and innumerable rhymes and chants which formed the heart of this culture. It thrived most of all amongst the children of the poor who enjoyed greater freedom from adult control and supervision on the streets, but it was also present, usually in a slightly more patchy and restrained form, among respectable and richer families. The single most important feature of this culture was its independence from the adult world – its home territory was the street, school playground and toilets, parks, tips, fields, any place where there was the chance of avoiding adult control.

The customs of this culture seem to have changed little over time. Many people remember that their first introduction to the body of the opposite sex was through the game of 'I'll show you mine if you show me yours'. This was a favourite game for children between the ages of about seven to ten. Ted Harrison, the son of a night street sweeper, born in 1904 and brought up in the East End of London, remembers playing this game around the beginning of the First World War:

> I was with Rosie and we were sitting on the mat just inside the passage of her house, 'cause it was raining and her mother kept on saying 'What are you doing?' and she'd say 'We're watching the raindrops.' But what she done, she said to me, 'I'll show you mine if you show me yours', and so we did that, we showed each other, and then we started exploring. And her mother kept on shouting out, 'What are you doing, Rosie?' 'Watching the raindrops, Mummy.' She was a bit posher than me; I was a little bit of a rough 'un and she had a nice ribbon in her hair, and she had drawers on. A lot of the girls I knew never had drawers on.

This mutual exploration was seen by children as completely natural, but girls who allowed gangs of young boys to fondle them often got reputations, the most common that they were 'daft'. Some may have been 'feeble-minded', but it is more likely that their reputation derived from the common prejudice against sexually active girls, probably learned from older boys and parents. George Gardner was the son of an overlooker in a Burnley cotton mill:

> Nobody told me anything about sex. It was towards the end of the First World War that I first became inquisitive. I was ten years old at the time and along with my mates from off our back street, we used to really enjoy our nightly sessions, sitting on the stone steps of Spender's weaving shed, supposedly staring up into the night sky watching for Zeppelins to come flying over Burnley, but really intent on looking at big Alice who was said to be a bit daft sitting in the middle of us and banging her well-formed bosom and bragging that she too could have a baby if she wanted to. Somehow I had an idea she was right because it was shortly after my elder sister got two lumps like Alice that she came to have a baby.

These early explorations were usually sexually innocent but by the teenage years they had become more explicitly sexual. Working-class boys and girls often developed a sexual interest before those from a middle-class background, mainly because they enjoyed much more freedom from adult control. Between the ages of fourteen to sixteen some were indulging in sexual play with whoever they were lucky enough to 'pick up' at parks, dances or on monkey runs – this was the term for streets where groups of young people paraded up and down, usually at weekends, in the hope of 'clicking' with somebody. Ted Harrison remembers some of his adventures as a fifteen year old in London:

A street scene in Northern England, around the turn of the century. Working-class children learned what little they knew about sex from friends on the streets

In 1919 after the war they started having dances in Victoria Park and I thought to myself, 'I'll have a go at that.' And we went there dancing and we got on with different girls dancing, and then I started to realize that there was something in this sex business. But I was more interested in what was above the belly button than what was below. I used to pick out girls with nice big tits, you know. I wasn't interested much in what was down below because I thought it was dirty. But above, I used to like to play with their tits and all that, used to squeeze 'em and push 'em and pull 'em around.

Many people, looking back, felt that their first sexual encounters were 'dirty' and that the furtive atmosphere in which they learned about their bodies encouraged a secret and unhealthy attitude towards sex. Much of the sexual slang of the shop floor, the pit and the office, filtered down, often through older boys at work, to provide the young with a crude and expressive ready-made vocabulary for everything to do with sex. There was some regional variation in this slang, but one common denominator was the slant of this language towards the idea of male conquest of a forbidden and rather frightening territory. John Binns remembers learning this slang in working-class Finsbury, North London, in the 1930s:

> To be crude we had all the usual words like shag and spunk and scrubber – I think that one, scrubber, was just coming at the time – but we had other ones as well, that I haven't heard anywhere else. If you boasted that you'd made love to a girl, and you usually hadn't, you'd say 'I had a bit of kife there.' If you'd felt a girl's breasts you'd say 'I had a good reef.' And if you'd felt her down below you'd say 'I got a handful of sprats.' Then there were lots of cruder words for things like oral sex, I remember we called that 'having a plate' or 'gumsucking'.

Along with this sexual slang went an array of sexual myths, some of them unpleasant, some of them simply misleading. For example, some girls learned on the streets or in playgrounds that they could become pregnant sitting on lavatory seats after boys, or by kissing or even touching a boy when menstruating. Another, perhaps more dangerous myth, was that sex standing up was fairly safe because the male sperm could not travel upwards. The sex education provided by the young for the young was clearly sometimes a case of the blind leading the blind. Its ignorance, guilt and sexism are perhaps not surprising, deriving as they did from the prevailing attitudes in the adult world. Yet despite its flaws, this independent culture continued to shape the sexual development of young people right through the first half of our century. This was because it provided them with a vocabulary, a knowledge and experience of sexuality that was denied elsewhere.

There was a conspiracy of silence about sex amongst most parents in most social classes. Sex was a taboo subject in most homes and this taboo persisted right up to the 1950s – and to some extent beyond. In 1949 the research organization Mass Observation completed a major sex survey – which was never published – that provides striking evidence of this taboo. They discovered that only 11 per cent of their sample received any sex instruction at all from their mother and a mere 6 per cent were given advice by their father. That parents could not bring themselves to talk honestly about sex to their children for so long is testimony not just to the strength of guilt-ridden Victorian attitudes on sexuality, but also to the power of the crude sexual culture which prevailed outside the home. This must often have provided the only real sexual vocabulary possessed by many parents which, because of its 'dirty' overtones, could not be used in a respectable home. There were also some practical considerations which entered into the parental silence on sex. Some working-class parents, for example, were prob-

A wash-and-brush-up for baby in 1908. Despite an appalling lack of facilities most poor parents went to great lengths to segregate washing and bathing, so that brothers and sisters rarely saw each other's naked bodies

ably frightened not just because of the possibility of a shameful and financially disastrous pregnancy in the family, but also of incest. This was a real problem in large families living in overcrowded houses where children shared beds and bedrooms. The taboo on this subject is so strong that even today very few are prepared to talk about it, but the reports of social reformers in late Victorian and Edwardian times show that incest was not uncommon amongst poor families. Ignorance was probably seen by parents as the best way of controlling and postponing the developing sexuality of their sons and daughters. Most mothers organized and segregated the dressing, bathing and washing of their children in such a way that sisters never saw the naked bodies of their brothers and vice versa. In overcrowded homes with few facilities this was a remarkable achievement. Unfortunately one of its effects was often to heighten children's anxiety about their sexuality.

The main burden of sexual responsibility – or more accurately the responsibility to avoid sex – seems to have been placed by parents on their daughters. The Mass Observation 1949 sex survey showed that daughters were more likely to receive sexual instruction than sons – and this was usually given by mothers. Propping up the responsibility was a strong undercurrent of anxiety and fear. It began with menstruation. The most common instructions given to girls entering sexual maturity was to hide their guilty secret and to avoid boys whenever they had a period. Marie Hill, the daughter of a carpenter, remembers the advice her mother gave her in Bristol during the 1920s:

> You could talk to your mother about any problem, but not sex, no fear. You never learnt nothing off of Mother. And with the majority of mothers that subject was taboo. She never even told us about when you had a period. You had a period, and Mother'd say, 'Oh you'll get that every month' and that was that. We'd say, 'There's blood' and she'd say, 'That ain't nothing, but keep away from the boys.' We used to make our own sanitary towels with pieces of towelling. There wasn't any bought sanitary towels then, nearly everybody did make their own. Put 'em in soak and mother did boil 'em and you used 'em again. Mother did put them in a bucket of water and she'd hide them from the boys, she'd tell you where to go and put them so that they wouldn't see them.

Sanitary towels, though invented in the 1890s, were rarely used by working-class women until after the Second World War – it proved too expensive – and most used and re-used torn off pieces of towel and sheeting. For some girls it must have often been difficult if not impossible to avoid smelling when they came on and this perhaps partly explains the shame that is attached to menstruation. However, there were deeper reasons for this shame and fear: for example, there was the centuries-old religious belief that menstruation was God's curse on the sin of Eve. This kind of attitude seems occasionally to have persisted not just in the church but among those involved in health care as Gladys Knight remembers from her schooldays in Edwardian Essex:

> I can remember I was pumping water and Mary was the monitor then. And I said to her, 'Oh,' I said, 'I've injured myself doing that pumping.' She said, 'What do you mean?' Of course I told her then. So she said, 'Don't you tell anybody but when you go to bed tonight you go and knock on matron's bedroom door and tell her.' So I knocked on the matron's door and she said, 'Oh that's the sin of woman, oh it's dreadful.' She said, 'Don't you ever tell anybody, that's a secret between yourself and nobody else.'

For Edwardian girls the average age at menarch was fifteen. By the 1960s it had reduced to thirteen. This meant that only a minority began their periods while at school. Some of those who did, however, found themselves sent home and exempted by doctors from the rest of their schooling. Until the First World War the medical profession widely saw menstruation as a time of illness and hysteria, when it was difficult to educate girls and inadvisable for them to work and play close to boys. The medical orthodoxy on menstruation changed after the war – it came to be viewed as a quite healthy and natural function of the body – but these old attitudes must have reinforced the anxiety and secrecy with which menstruation and sexual maturation were treated in many homes. Menstruation was still a secret source of shame in many families well into the inter-war years. Babs Pringle, the daughter of a policeman and Irish Catholic mother, remembers how periods were treated in her home in Grimsby in the 1930s:

> I once found some stained towels in the laundry basket and naturally asked what it was. There was no such thing as sanitary towels; we used old strips of sheet. I can still recall the utter confusion on my mother's face when she said, 'Your sister has had a nosebleed.' So this was the sort of dreadful constraints we had to put up with. Needless to say when I did start periods it was a terrible shock. I thought I was dying. I was also terrified when I grew hair on my body and spent many shameful secret hours trying to cut it off as I thought I was the only one to have this.

As a result of the lack of sex instruction in most late Victorian and Edwardian homes some seem to have genuinely believed that babies were brought by doctors in their black bags or were found under gooseberry bushes or were brought by storks. Considerable numbers of women faced pregnancy and childbirth with no knowledge of what was about to happen to their bodies. However, beginning in the 1900s and especially from the 1920s onwards there does seem to have been a more serious attempt by a minority of parents to provide some basic sexual instruction, especially for girls, more out of fear than anything else. But it was still learning laced with Victorian taboos about sex for pleasure and sex before marriage. Lady Marguerite Tangye remembers the advice given by her mother in the mid-1920s:

ARE THERE DAYS IN THE MONTH YOU DREAD?

SUN 1 8 15 22 29

MON

I'M SORRY I CAN'T COME DEAR, I'M IN SUCH PAIN I HAVE HAD TO GO TO BED

MARY YOU REALLY MUST GET SOME **ANTI-KAMNIA** TABLETS. TAKE ONE OR TWO AND YOU'LL FEEL FINE IN A FEW MINUTES

Pains no Woman need endure

Too ill to dance, prostrate with pain for days each month; life is too short for such a sacrifice. Nor is it necessary, since "Anti-Kamnia" has made 'painless periods' an accomplished fact.

If indisposition for you means unbearable headaches, and depressing pains, you will find an unfailing remedy in "Anti-Kamnia". At the first symptom of pain take one or two tablets. The suffering you

have learned to dread will pass you by and you will be fit and able to keep all your engagements as usual. "Anti-Kamnia" is the remedy most extensively prescribed by physicians and recommended by nurses, because of its wonderful power to relieve pain and the fact that it does not disturb the natural action of the female system in the slightest. Why not get the tablets to-day and have them in readiness?

AK **Anti-Kamnia**
BRAND ANALGESIC TABLETS
1/3 per box. Of Chemists only.
ALWAYS SURE — ALWAYS SAFE

1930s advert for 'painless periods'. Menstruation at this time was surrounded by great anxiety and guilt

She sat down with me and tried to explain the mechanics and I looked at her and saw she was very embarrassed and I wasn't really listening. And so, I must have been thirteen, I knew what she'd said but it had no relation whatsoever to the rest of my life. So when I grew up I knew in theory and yet I knew nothing, very difficult to explain. I think what was left out was desire, lust, the feeling a man had when he raped someone, this overwhelming drive, that was left out totally. What was told you was the mechanics of it. And so you thought, 'That's simple, that's nothing', what you didn't realize was the big drive. The desire is what causes the trouble. She would say, 'It's either sacred or disgusting.' That was her idea of it, you either did it in a sacred way because you wanted a baby or it was disgusting and not to be mentioned. Even to romance, with a man singing under your window, everything to do with that sort of thing was disgusting. That's what she told me. I didn't take any notice at all.

An Edwardian postcard. Lack of sex instruction meant that some people genuinely believed that babies were brought by storks or found under gooseberry bushes

Often parents waited until just before their daughters' wedding before giving them any advice. The logic of this was that it was only then that a daughter, whom they assumed to be a virgin, would need any knowledge of sex. Betty Tucker, the daughter of a Stoke-on-Trent railwayman who married in the late 1950s, received her one and only piece of sexual advice from her father on the way to her wedding. 'My dear dad told me nothing but in the taxi going to church he gave me a tin of vaseline because he said I might be a bit sore that night.' Unbeknown to her father she had long lost her virginity.

The most common conversation with daughters about sex, however, usually took the form of a threat about the dire consequences of 'getting into trouble'. The warning to the daughter, often couched in euphemisms, was that she would be sent to the workhouse should she get pregnant. Occasionally, it seems, girls were so innocent that they had no idea of the meaning of this threat as Daphne Richards, who began courting in Barnsley during the early 1930s, remembers. 'When I first started courting – as we called it – my father said to me, "If you bring any trouble home you will go in the workhouse, so keep yourself clean." I hadn't a clue what he meant so I just got bathed every day.' When daughters eventually discovered the realities of sex, often from girl-friends or boyfriends, some were shocked and felt that their trust had been betrayed by their parents. The guilt and secrecy with which the facts of life had been hidden from them for so many years sometimes made sex appear as distasteful to them as it was to their parents. This was one way in which sexual guilt seems to have been transmitted from one generation to the next.

Whereas most daughters were given warnings about the dangers of sex, and increasingly from the inter-war years onwards even some moralistic instruction in the workings of their bodies, there was far less attention paid by parents to sexual advice for their sons. Few remember any talk or lecture on sex by either their mother or father. Clearly greater sexual freedom was given to boys and this also tended to be reflected in their being allowed out at night more often – without supervision or chaperone – and allowed back later than their sisters. However, they were certainly not encouraged to sow their wild oats: parents who discovered that their son was sexually active would be very disapproving and pressure was put on sons who got girls 'into trouble' to marry them. The concern with family respectability usually far outweighed the double standard when it came to making a moral judgment about a son's sexual behaviour.

Although most sons and daughters found it difficult or impossible to approach their parents over sexual matters, there were sometimes other relatives with whom they could share their problems. There was a recurrent tendency for young people to turn to a favourite uncle, aunt, gran or granddad for sexual advice. Indeed these relatives sometimes actually initiated the sexual discussion. Being one step removed from the anxiety and fear that stopped so many parents from giving matter-of-fact advice to their sons and daughters on sex, they were able to talk much more openly and honestly. This intimacy could occasionally generate relationships, say between granddaughters and grans, that were actually closer and more affectionate than those between daughters and mothers. Winnie Stradling, the daughter of a wheelwright, born in 1901 in Peckham, South London, was one of eight children brought up on the bread line:

She was a prude, yes, very prudish my mother. And one day I asked her a question as I was getting on and she just smacked my face, and it was to do with me, myself and she would never tell you anything you see, you had to learn all your things about anything from other girls. You couldn't, and you know it wasn't really fair. All the information that I ever got I got, thank God I had a very wonderful grandma. And do you know, perhaps it's not right to say it, but I loved my grandma much more than I loved my mother. My grandma was the dearest lady, to this day I've never met another lady like her. She used to have the patience of a saint and when I was beginning to grow up and I used to visit her, she used to say to me, 'Come and sit down, Duckie.' Used to go and sit down. 'Getting a big girl now,' she'd say. 'Well you know what you've got to do, you've got to be careful you know.' And I used to look at her. So she said, 'You've been talking to the girls?' And I used to say, 'Yes.' 'Well,' she said, 'listen. And if there's anything you don't understand, I know your mother won't tell you, you come and tell gran.' And I used to. I learned quite a lot from my grandma. . . . When I went to work during the First World War when I was sixteen, I was shocked when I heard them sitting there talking and one of them said, 'Look at her with her mouth wide open.' I couldn't believe what they said, I couldn't believe it. I kept thinking about it, thinking about it, and I went – I'll go to my grandma. And she knew, when she saw my face, there was something wrong. Said, 'What's the matter, love?' So I told her. So she says, 'Come here, sit down.' Put her arm round me. 'Now,' she said, 'they've told you in a very bald way, that's wicked,' she said. 'Yes, yes, the baby is born like that.' So I said, 'Well, how does it get there?' So there's my grandma telling me the difference between a girl and a boy, and the way she put it, she ought to have been alive today, she could have taught them how to tell people about sex. And do you know I thought when she told me and how she explained it to me, not like some people think it's dirty, I thought it was wonderful. I did really.

The advice given by well-meaning relatives would more often than not be heavily loaded with euphemisms; a very good example of this is the tip on withdrawal that was given to Bill Sides, the son of a miner brought up in an East Durham mining village during the 1920s and 1930s:

47

My aunt was my source for information, advice and tips, although I very much doubt if she told her own family anything. I must emphasize she was not crude or vulgar, though she had some strange sayings. One bit of advice was 'If you touch that girl', meaning sex, 'treat it as a bus ride. Jump off the bus one stop before the one you want.' The penny did not drop regarding that advice for a long, long time.

While a few kind relatives were striving to educate their nieces and grandchildren, the cause of sexual enlightenment amongst the young was certainly not advanced by the official schooling system. Sex education was simply not recognized on the curriculum of most schools, whether state, public or private, until the post-war years. In 1914, for instance, the London County Council banned sex instruction from elementary schools in the capital, a ban which remained in force until after the Second World War. There were some official lectures and films provided in schools during the inter-war years by the Social Purity and Hygiene Movement, but these were little more than propaganda warning the young of the moral and physical dangers of promiscuity and venereal disease. Mass Observation's sex survey found that less than 10 per cent of those who attended schools before the 1920s remembered being given any instruction at all in the classroom. Although some schools introduced basic sex instruction into biology lessons from the 1920s onwards it was usually of a complex physiological type which was difficult to understand and which fell short of describing the sex act. Discussion of sex in schools actually went against the grain of the schooling system, especially for older pupils, during the first half of our century, for the main emphasis was on encouraging obedience, discipline and restraint. In this formal atmosphere any mention of sex was taboo, not least because it was feared it might be a disruptive influence. The dominant educational theories of the period claimed that segregation either into single sex schools or a degree of sex segregation in mixed schools was particularly advantageous in avoiding potentially dangerous contact between the sexes at a vulnerable age. Around a half of all state elementary schools and three-quarters of state secondary schools remained single sex until after the Second World War. And grammar and public schools remained predominantly single sex until the last few decades when coeducation became fashionable.

In this segregated system the independent culture of the young took on a new and subversive significance. For illicit contact between girls and boys was often a serious breach of discipline. Many Edwardian school teachers would cane children found guilty of such minor offences as sending love letters, kissing, ogling or even just looking at members of the opposite sex while at school. In private and public schools secret meetings with boyfriends or girlfriends – especially if they occurred after curfews – were often punished by expulsion.

A girls' school in 1912. Most schools in Edwardian Britain were sex segregated, partly to postpone sexual interest and maturation

However, teachers found it very difficult to control larking about between boys and girls and illicit affairs because it was – if nothing else – an easy way of injecting interest and excitement into the monotonous school routine. This battle between teachers and pupils over proper conduct between the sexes continued unabated during the inter-war years. Bert Mullen went to school in Bristol during the 1930s:

As far as sex education was concerned, until the time I was fourteen when I left elementary school, sex was taboo, there was no mention of the subject whatsoever. I remember once, I was in a mixed school for a while called Alexandra Park at Fishponds, there were girls and boys at different classes, and one girl in particular was sweet on me and sent me a note to say that she had some cakes, some apple dumplings for me which she'd made in her cookery class. And this note was found by one of the masters and it was read out to the entire school the following morning as a big joke. 'Dear Bert, I have some apple dumplings for you, will see you after school,' something like that. I felt a bit soft, it was a huge joke among the pupils for a few days until it died a natural death.

Any sexual contact between older boys and girls on the school

49

premises was treated as a much more serious offence. The punishment for this in the inter-war school was often a sadistic beating which harked back to the more severe punishments of Edwardian days. Bill Phillips attended an elementary school in the East End of London in the 1920s:

> It was a mixed school and you know what girls are, they come up and want to lark about with you, and I got this girl behind the shed. Course I didn't know what sex was, it was just feeling one another sort of thing. And I got caught behind the shed by the master and he had me in front of the class and he said, 'Right, I'm going to make an example of you,' he said, 'I'm going to stop this once and for all.' And he took me in the room, took my trousers down, bare backside, and caned me, and I couldn't sit down for a week. He wanted to cane me in front of the class but the Headmaster said 'Do it properly, take him in the room and take his trousers down,' because he couldn't take my trousers down in front of the class.'

What some mixed schools seem to have feared most of all were assaults on girls. These must have happened from time to time and were a proper cause for concern, but in some schools there seems to have been a hysterical overreaction to what was in fact just innocent horseplay and larking about between boys and girls. Ray Rochford attended a Catholic school in Salford, Manchester, during the 1930s:

> This school I went to, they had a big garden, and they didn't believe in keeping kids idle as we had to do the weeding for the priest in summertime, once a week. I remember this day, I was ready for leaving, I was getting on for fourteen and he took us out, about six boys and six girls, and the girls were doing the watering, and we were doing the weeding, kneeling down. And I remember this vividly: there was a tomboy girl, her name was Brenda; she could climb, run, fight, swim. I was knelt down and she poured this water down my neck. I grabbed her and I threw her down and I was banging her. But her frock came over her hips and she had no knickers on. Now a lot of girls didn't wear underclothes then – I never did. This housekeeper, she could see me through the window and she ran down shouting, and I didn't know, this girl was kicking her legs in the air and she must have been showing everything. So the priest come up. 'What are you playing at, what are you doing?' He took me in the Presbytery. 'What did you do to that girl?' I said, 'I was fighting her.' 'No, you wasn't.' So they sent the girl home and next day I was called out into the middle of the class, this was the humiliating part. Now this mother had sent this girl to school with no knickers on but she must have told the girl, 'Tell 'em you had knickers on,' you see, because she'd be ashamed for the neighbours to know. So when they asked her she

said, 'I had knickers on when I came to school,' so naturally I'd taken them off, hadn't I, see. And I got six of the cane on each hand, but it wasn't the pain that hurt. My mother was ashamed of me and she didn't believe me. Funnily enough, my father did, he believed me, but Mother didn't. She said, 'I'll have to go down and see Mrs Hopwood.' 'Oh, Raymond,' she said, 'I don't know how I'm going to live this down.' She was more concerned about her position in the street, what all the neighbours thought. But I didn't know what I'd done wrong and I kept saying 'We were just fighting.' 'No you wasn't,' she said. 'You were doing something else.' I thought what else could I do. But that was the situation you got into, this horrific accusation. I hadn't a clue why I was being punished.

A similar kind of segregation and supervision of contact between the sexes featured in most of the clubs and organizations that young people joined in their spare time. From late Victorian times onwards there was an explosion of youth movements organized by adults to try to 'improve' the character of the young in their leisure hours. Some, like the Band of Hope, Church Lads' Brigades, the YMCA and the Girls' Friendly Societies, were overtly the work of the church. Others, like the Boys' Brigades, the Boy Scouts and the Girl Guides, though partly inspired by religious motives, created a much more independent image and organization which was more attractive to young people bored with the church. What these movements shared was an anxiety and concern with the moral and physical condition of young people in the new industrial age. They were involved in a civilizing mission to instil values of patriotic and religious duty, discipline and higher moral standards into young people, and in particular working-class youth. Generations of Brigade leaders and Scout masters believed that for this crusade to be successful they would have to tackle what they saw as one of the main evils corrupting young minds and bodies – sex. Masturbation, flirting, larking about and promiscuity were seen as terrible moral dangers which diverted youth from more noble ideals like service to king and country. The organization of these youth movements which were invariably sex segregated and disapproving of serious relationships between boys and girls, reflects this concern.

In terms of their membership these movements were remarkably successful. Several million young people passed through the ranks of these organizations during their heyday between the 1880s and the 1930s. But although they enjoyed a hold over many young people into their late teens their success in moulding the minds of young people should not be exaggerated. Most boys and girls joined to take part in the musical, sporting and holiday activities that these youth movements offered. Interviews suggest that they were far less serious about the compulsory church services, moral lectures and adult supervision which came as part of the package. Indeed, here again, the deep-rooted

culture of the young provided a sexual freedom and independence which the propaganda and sex segregation of the youth movements was never able to penetrate fully. Mercifully there were probably few whose emerging sexuality was crushed as brutally as that of Albert Mitchell, the son of a stern Victorian clerk brought up in Manchester during the inter-war years:

Boy Scouts in action during 'bob-a-job' week before the First World War. Sex-segregated organizations like this often disapproved of – and tried to prevent – serious relationships developing between boys and girls during the early teens

> I was born in 1921 and went to a Church of England school where we spent lots of time singing hymns. And I went to Boy Scouts and Sunday school, and then to secondary school where boys were segregated from girls in a separate building and thoroughly isolated. I was completely inhibited, confused and unable to cope with any sort of relationship with the opposite sex in spite of strong profound and inexplicable emotions stirring within me. My parents strictly enforced my attendance at church school, church choir, Boy Scouts, church and Sunday school I was inculcated with dogma about 'the sins of the flesh', 'adultery and fornication', 'the story of Adam and Eve', 'thou shalt not commit adultery', 'the doom of Sodom and Gomorrah', and during my

working days and years in the armed forces from 1938 to 1943 I was completely ignorant of sex and unable to cope or find any oulet for the forces surging within me. I really believed then, deep within me, that sex was a sin of a profound and terrible nature. This disturbance caused me some troubles which interfered with my education and talents in my daily job and tasks as deep down I was tormented by clashing emotions, and my emotions struggled against the fear and dogmas of my upbringing. During my nineteenth and twentieth years I might say I fell in love, as far as I was able, with two young ladies, but both affairs were completely platonic and caused me great anguish, although I realize now that the females concerned wanted rather a deeper relationship. I was completely unable to release my deeper feelings in any way and transfer them into the warmth of a human relationship. Both those associations ended.

The church wielded immense power on matters of sexual morality during the first half of our century and this power frequently impinged on the lives of the young. The Catholic church, for example, took a particularly hard and unashamedly repressive line on sex and the pressure it put on the young to conform to a Christian ideal was invariably backed up by family and community alike. The little evidence we have – for example, low illegitimacy rates amongst Irish Catholics – suggest that the Catholic church was particularly successful in inculcating a deep fear of sex before marriage. This control over the sexual behaviour of young people was even more remarkable given the repeated waves of mass migration from Ireland into Britain from Victorian times onwards. Migration of this sort by young single men and women is often associated with a loosening of controls on sexuality. John Neary was brought up in the tiny village of Culmore in County Mayo, and left in 1926 to tramp across Britain working as a navvy on building sites. In 1930 he settled down in Dagenham, Essex, married a local girl and spent the rest of his working life at the Ford motor company. His testimony gives us an insight into how Catholic taboos on sex, once established in childhood, survived the passage to Britain and were reinforced wherever Irish Catholics settled.

At a very young age you had to go to Confession, it was started about six or seven, and every Saturday morning the kids would all go to confess. But when you went to Confession, there were no holds barred; they asked you straight out and you were that scared you told them everything. And if you chased little girls down the lane, they were scared too, they had to tell it. And the mothers were briefed. So that was how there was very very little of sex, because we was drilled from the early days. We had people go round that was church missionaries, tough men, and what the priests didn't do, they did and they took it further. And they was really very intimate and they used to go round the houses in the

Two slides from a 'sex education' show around the turn of the century. The first represents sexual innocence and purity. The second represents sexual experience and corruption

54

village to make sure that everybody went to Confession. At Confession the priest would say, 'Did you have anything to do with the local girls?' 'Did you ever kiss them?' 'Yes.' 'Did you kiss them more than once?' 'Yes.' 'Did you feel their body? Tell me the truth, yes or no, answer, quick!' And if you said yes there was noise, he had a verbal attack on you. And the people lining up to go into the Confession box, they used to be scared to go in there. . . . It persisted because most of the priests in the churches here in Britain were Irish, or quite a lot of them, they carried on where the other Irish priests left off. And of course when I came here, a lot of my mates were church-goers and if you didn't go to church they used to say 'He never went to church or Confession.' The priest used to recommend that you went to lodge in Catholic houses so that the landlady there would drill you anyway. It was a way of life, it was far deeper than anyone outside the Catholic church could realize. We used to go to church on Sunday, Sunday night and Thursday. And Saturday night was Confession. So if you wanted a girlfriend on the quiet you had to be very quick to find her during the week.

If the anxious youth, inquisitive to discover what sex was all about, fell upon a sex manual, he or she could still not escape from the influence of a repressive Christian morality. The church provided more than its fair share of authors of sex manuals and even when writers had no direct attachment to the church, they invariably served up large moral helpings of how and why not to indulge in sex. One of the most extraordinary features of these sex manuals, especially those written between the 1850s and the 1920s, was the attack that they launched on the evils of masturbation. This was in part a reflection of the medical orthodoxy of the day which claimed that 'self-abuse' – 'the solitary vice' or 'the secret sin' as it was known – had seriously damaging effects on the mind and the body. With very little evidence, a succession of clergymen, doctors and psychiatrists claimed that masturbation was the cause of many ailments and diseases – blindness, baldness, epilepsy and impotence were those most commonly mentioned, and it could even, it was claimed, lead to insanity. Professor G. Stanley Hall, the world's leading authority on adolescence, described self-abuse in 1911 as an 'insidious disease', 'the scourge of the human race' and 'an influence that seems to spring from the Prince of Darkness'. Masturbation was also immoral not least because it wasted valuable sperm which needed to be saved and stored in order to make healthy babies and contribute to the strength and purity of the race. Baden Powell warned Boy Scouts in *Rovering to Success* that:

> it cheats semen getting its full chance of making up the strong manly man you would otherwise be. . . . You are throwing away the seed that has been handed down to you as a trust instead of keeping it and ripening it for bringing a son to you later on.

The habit was believed to be most widespread among boys but large numbers of girls were also infected – a cause for much concern because it threatened the popular view of the sexless, morally pure woman who was only interested in sex as a means of having babies. The most popular cure was cold baths, long walks and prayer. The Reverend W. H. Elliott, writing in 1924, helpfully advised that the masturbator 'must be taught the use of ejaculatory prayer at the moment of temptation; just when the stress comes he should say "Oh God, keep me pure", or "Oh my God, give me strength to resist temptation."'

It is difficult to assess what impact this crusade had on boys and girls growing up in late Victorian and Edwardian times. Although Baden Powell's warning against self-abuse in *Rovering to Success* may well have been read by a quarter of a million Boy Scouts, most other sex manuals of the times had quite small circulations and were much more likely to have been read by youth leaders or clergymen who used them as the basis for talks and lectures to the young. We know little about how they responded to this propaganda but the little evidence that exists suggests that it heightened their fear and anxiety without necessarily leading them to abandon the habit. 'The solitary vice' and the difficulty of giving it up was a common source of correspondence on the problem pages of boys' comics like the *Boy's Own Newspaper* around the turn of the century. When Marie Stopes rose to fame in the 1920s she received a number of letters from 'addicts' who were extremely disturbed about their habit. And Mass Observation in its sex report of 1949 found evidence that in the past there had been a high level of anxiety about masturbation. One man born in the 1880s remembered:

> I had no sex education, what I picked up was from bigger boys in a vulgar way. From them I learned masturbation which nearly ruined me; fortunately someone knew what I was about and put a leaflet my way which I read and took to heart – just in time to prevent me from becoming a waster or imbecile. That was the only bit of advice I ever had.

Living memory from the inter-war years suggests that masturbation, though still strongly disapproved of by parents and moral reformers, was being treated in a slightly more relaxed way. Most sex manuals and lectures were by this time increasingly turning to promiscuity and venereal disease as the real enemies, and this may have helped to create a slightly less oppressive atmosphere about 'the solitary vice'. A number of interviewees who went to grammar or public school between the wars recalled that masturbation was quite common amongst the boys in toilets, gyms and dormitories and that no great feelings of guilt were associated with it. Indeed boys from all backgrounds who indulged in masturbation did not feel ashamed in the way that they might have done thirty or forty years before, even if they were caught in the act. Nathan Stone, the son of a blade grinder, grew up in inter-war Sheffield:

An Edwardian sex manual for 'working mothers'. Note the warning, quite common at the time, in the top left-hand corner

☞ **For private reading. Not to be left about.**

Things we must tell our Girls

Written for Working Mothers

BY

CLARE GOSLETT

Price Fourpence
By post, Fivepence

Published by
ALLMAN & SON, LIMITED
67, NEW OXFORD STREET, LONDON, W.C.

Or to be obtained of
Mrs. CLARE GOSLETT, Kenilworth House, Ealing, W.

When I was thirteen I had a very funny sensation. I got a slight burning sensation in my little willie. I wondered what was the matter so I went to the lavvie which was outside in the backyard and shared by two families. I touched my willie and it started to grow. I kept on touching and suddenly it spit at me. I looked at the gooey result and felt sick as a pig and dirty all over. Then the door opened and my mother came in. She seemed to know automatically what was happening, gave me a clip on the earhole and said, 'Nathan, that'll send thee blind if tha does it too thisen too often.' That saying seemed to stop me abusing myself in later life as often as some of my mates. They would do it till they went red in the face and quite exhausted. Good old mum.

Even when boys were lectured at school or in youth clubs about the dangers of masturbation, the language used was often so obtuse and euphemistic that they didn't understand what the warning was about. Ray Rochford was brought up in a slum area of Salford near Manchester in the 1930s:

People in authority, they would pontificate about the dangers of self-indulgence – we naturally thought that meant over-eating – and self-abuse – which of course we thought meant hitting yourself with a hammer. It used to go straight over our heads. Now if they had said, 'Don't wank or toss yourself off', we would have got the message. Not that it would have made the slightest difference to us. It was too enjoyable to stop, besides it was the only one pleasure that didn't cost anything. I can remember a friend stating to us all at one communal wank that he earnestly wished that the 'pipe of prick' was a mile long when he was coming. I guess that just about sums it all up.

During the inter-war years the sex manual began to change in a way which provided at least a few young people with practical information about the sex act itself. The controversial books written by pioneer birth-controller Marie Stopes in the 1920s, which sold hundreds of thousands of copies, were some of the first to provide explicit descriptions of sexual intercourse. Despite this, the dominant tradition remained the old moralistic one of thundering against the moral and physical damage of sex before marriage, while – perhaps not surprisingly – providing no information on how to do it. Often the line was drawn at analogies with reproduction in plants and animals. For example, the Reverend H. H. Birley's sex instruction manual of 1921 explained reproduction through an illustrated discussion of 'the male and female parts in primrose and vegetable marrow'.

But even though there were now more practical sex books on the market young people must have found it extremely difficult to actually get them to read. This is reflected in the fact that Mass Observation's sex survey in 1949 discovered that only 8 per cent of its sample had learned about the facts of life through reading a sex manual. Part of the problem was that the books containing explicit information were written for married couples. Here, for example, is a sample of the titles of sex manuals written by Marie Stopes: *Wise Parenthood: A Book for Married People* (1918), *Radiant Motherhood* (1920) and *Married Love* (1923). With titles like these young people – in the very different moral atmosphere of the inter-war years – may well have had difficulty buying them from bookshops or borrowing them from libraries. Many sex manuals stated that they were for married couples, school teachers or whoever. On the dust jacket of Dr Eustace Chesser's *Love Without Fear* (1941), for example, was the following message:

> The author has written this book for those who are married or about to be married and in this connection the bookseller's co-operation is requested.

Living memory suggests that older boys and girls bought or borrowed books and showed them, secretly, to younger ones. Also some sympathetic and broad-minded relatives secretly gave or lent useful sex manuals to teenage boys and girls. Bill Sides was the lucky recipient of such a book in his East Durham mining village in the 1930s:

> My aunty supplied a book written by Doctor Marie Stopes with the warning do not get caught reading it at home, and to keep it hidden at all times. A loose cover off a cowboy novel solved that problem. All advice was given under the Official Secrets Act, the informant's name was never to be disclosed!

Occasionally children and young people might stumble across a sex manual kept by their parents at home and read it. John Binns remembers such an episode happening when he was just eleven years old:

> I was playing about with a little girl, touching her in between her legs when all of a sudden, wallop! To be rude, I came me lot. And it frightened the life out of me. No one had ever told us this sort of thing could happen. I ran upstairs being dressed as you can imagine, it was quite messy. I thought I was ill, queer, there's something wrong. And after that I never saw that girl again even though she only lived a few turnings away from me; I just couldn't face her. I was possibly ashamed, I never told anyone, never! I was frightened. Because in my days you weren't given the birds and bees story so to speak, you more or less had to find out your own way. And I found out by going through my mother's dressing table one time, and I saw this book and it had various diagrams for the penis and vaginas, which, although I knew about it I didn't realize they could be drawn or explained. My sister was older than me so I never saw that kind of thing and years ago you were kept apart. And when I saw this book it opened my eyes you know. Then I realized that what I did was probably a normal function and I was

quite happy after that, reading that it opened my eyes. And instead of listening to the tales of other boys – as kids you used to stretch a point, you always thought that when the doctor came with the black bag and all of a sudden you heard some squealing, you thought he brought the baby with him, you didn't realize, or some used to say it came out of the woman's backside – and that completely put my mind at rest, I knew exactly how babies were formed, and that was quite a good thing for me.

There was one last hope for young people eager for practical information about sex – the sex shop. These places variously known as sex shops, rubber stores or surgical supply stores, were usually small seedy establishments selling a variety of medical goods, quack cures, rubber wear and contraceptives. Most towns and cities had a few such shops. There were often close connections between these sex shops and the underworld of backstreet abortions, prostitution and pornography. Their great attraction for the young was that some of the proprietors or shop assistants would, according to interviewees, often provide practical, matter-of-fact information on sexual matters to anyone who inquired – with no questions asked and no moral lectures. They were often given advice on contraception and the sex act that no doctor or teacher would ever dream of revealing to a young unmarried person – and possibly simply did not know anyway because there was a high level of ignorance of sex in both these professions during the inter-war years. Stan Hall's family ran the 'surgical supply stores' in Chesterfield between the early 1920s and the 1950s. Most of the young customers were 'very clever types' who wanted more information than they had been told in biology lessons:

> I was seen by grammar school types and high school females. It was being far too cheeky to approach their own family doctor. A great many contraceptive firms would produce excellent leaflets and some shops soon had a great many books which could be read. I had many books which were very costly and I loaned them out to particular grammar school lads and lasses. Some soon became very knowledgeable indeed and sometimes I was pushed to know how to answer some of their queries. There were some lads and they brought their girlfriends into the shop for a session and they were able to see the various caps which were sold and the condoms on offer. I remember one knowledgeable lad and his girlfriend who took away a lot of books used to read them together in their dinner hour in a local park or the fields nearby.

The last and perhaps most important group of educators of young people into the mysteries of sex were workmates. For the working-class young the culture of the factory floor and the pit represented a tougher and more adult version of their own independent street culture. There was often 'bad language', 'dirty' jokes and stories of sexual adventures

Apprentices share a joke in an iron foundry in the North East of England during the 1930s. Many young lads were initiated into the mysteries of sex by their workmates

in abundance. The transition into adulthood was ritualized in many work places in initiation rituals for apprentices and new boys and new girls, in which young workers would be ritually humiliated. There was often a strong sexual element in this humiliation. Most commonly the victim's clothes would be taken off and his or her genitals smeared with oil, tar or grease. This was partly a statement to everyone that the 'virgin' boy or girl had now arrived into the adult world and would have to face up to its realities – and one of these realities was sex. This exposure to the 'reality' of the shop floor was sometimes quite shocking, especially to those who had had a fairly sheltered upbringing, because there was a strong element of sexual violence in its culture. The sexual initiation of young boys was traditionally undertaken by older women and it often seems to have given rise to a desire amongst the boys to 'get their own back' on girls through sexual conquest, thus reinforcing the sexism of the shop floor. Bill Phillips began work in an East End factory in the early 1920s.

> I went to work in the factory and there were loads of women there and me being the only boy there, one day they says to me, 'Go down the cellar and get something.' I went down and next thing I knew they all jumped on me, got me down, got me trousers down, played with it, in fact I didn't know what was happening I thought

I was in a new world. They all massaged me, about six of them give me a massage, and then that finished and they all painted it with black tar. And when I went home, I went home crying to my mother and I said to her, 'I don't like working at that factory.' And she said 'Why?' So I said, I couldn't tell her what happened, I said, 'The women swear.' So she said, 'Take no notice of them.' Really I was shocked because it was something that never happened to me before. And of course from then onwards I decided I would have my own back on women, which I did.

Once over the initial shock of entering the world of work many young people enjoyed the more open sexual atmosphere of the shop floor which for all its teasing, crudity and sexism provided a preferable alternative to the sexual secrecy of home and school. In a sense this culture often helped working-class youth to become more 'knowledge-able' more quickly about sex than those from a middle-class back-ground who remained at school, college and university into their later teens and early twenties. They too would learn more about sex from more experienced colleagues in offices when they were slightly older, though it would usually be done in a more discreet and private way, and there was nothing to compare with the sexual initiations characteristic of the factory. Testimony to the continuing influence of the workplace together with the independent culture of youth as a means of learning about sex, is provided by Mass Observation's survey of 1949. The great majority of those questioned said that they had learned most of what they knew about sex by 'picking it up' from workmates and friends.

If the workplace was in a sense the finishing school for sexual education, the knowledge that it imparted was studded with ignorance, fear and myth. The bravado and boasting was partly a cover for the fact that when away from the pally atmosphere of the factory and the office, courting couples and young lovers were still lacking in a basic sex education. If they could overcome their anxiety they would teach themselves through trial and error in their relationships. But where errors occurred – as they frequently did – they could have appalling consequences, especially for the young woman. Though not as ignor-ant as has often been thought, they entered adult life dangerously ill-equipped to cope with sexual experience, particularly sex before marriage.

3

THE ROAD TO RUIN

Rose Crompton is a sprightly eighty-nine year old with sparkling brown eyes and a great sense of humour. She talks in a soft West Midlands accent and everyone who knows her seems to speak to her as a friend. The only really surprising thing about Rose – apart from her unusual alertness for someone so old – is that she has spent her entire life since the age of eighteen in an institution. This life sentence, most of which she has spent in mental hospitals of various sorts, began when her grandmother sent her to the workhouse after she discovered she was pregnant with an illegitimate child. In fact, she had been raped:

> I come home from night school and it was dark and foggy, and I went home by myself. And I said to this boy, 'Would you mind taking me along the canal side?' I was frightened to death I'd get drowned, you know. He got me by the wall. I says 'Go on, get away, I don't want any children. You're only a young chap. I don't want you.' I says, 'I'll have to go to the workhouse.' And he got me against the wall. Oh, I did cry. I says, 'Don't you dare do that dirty trick to me.' He took me home all right then he says, 'Good night.' I says, 'Yes, after you've done the deed. Take me to your mother and your dad's, it's your child. You've raped me.' He said, 'Oh, I daren't take you home to me mother and my dad.' 'No,' I says, 'because you've done a bad deed.' If I'd known I could have asked a policeman, because all the policemen knew me in West Bromwich. I didn't see one about see. I says 'If you get me into trouble you'll have to pay for the child,' but he didn't pay for it. He never even took me to his people.

Later when Rose discovered she was pregnant she told her parents:

> I told my mother and my grandma said, 'What's her talking about, our Elizabeth? Oh, her's going daft.' I said, 'Well, if you want to know, I've got a tumour.' I knowed I hadn't. They said, 'You'll have to go to the doctor.' But I cried, and me grandma cried. I said, 'Well, I didn't ask for trouble,' I said, 'I asked for a kindness and that's what I got, rape.' The doctor said, 'What can I do for you, Rose?' 'Well,' I says, 'I've got into trouble.' He says I've got to go to the workhouse. 'Who says?' I ask. 'Your grandma.' 'I'm not going,' I says. 'I'll have the baby here at home.' 'You won't!' mother said. 'To the workhouse you'll go!' Mother cried. She sent me in. I got my clothes ready, waved goodbye. 'I hope it's

A Church Army propaganda wagon in the 1920s warns passers-by of the sins of the flesh

taught you a lesson.' I says, 'You'll want me some time. God'll be good to me some day.'

Rose's tragic misfortune was to continue, however. She was removed from the workhouse and placed in a local mental hospital. Her story is testimony to the terrible victimization of young women who bore illegitimate children. She was one of countless thousands who were locked away in reformatories and mental hospitals under a pernicious piece of legislation – the Mental Deficiency Act of 1913. This gave wide-ranging powers to local authorities to certify pregnant women who were homeless, destitute or, in official eyes, 'immoral', and detain them indefinitely. The law fell most heavily on destitute young women who were themselves illegitimate – as was Rose – for according to fashionable eugenic theories of the time they and their children were thought to be hereditarily feeble-minded. In 1917 Rose gave birth to a baby daughter. She too was placed in institutional care as was the custom for illegitimate children of mothers classified as mentally subnormal. She died at the age of two. By this time Rose had been recruited as an unwaged toilet cleaner and she would continue her serf-like duties in the institutions where she was placed in custody for the next half century. Like many, she became institutionalized into a self-contained world of locked wards, uniforms and sewing classes: 'It just came in me mind. I thought I shall never get out into the world now. But still I was happy. I thought, well, I'm safer here than outside. Well, you are, aren't you?'

Some were released in the late 1950s when the original legislation was repealed and a gradual liberalization of mental hospitals got under way. By then, however, many of the victims of the Act were old and institutionalized and most would end their days in the wards where they had for so long been imprisoned. Just a few survivors, like Rose, remain – reminders of an age when the stigma of bearing an illegitimate child was so great that it was possible to think of the poor pregnant victims as mentally defective or even insane. Rose's experience was among the worst, for not all young women who had babies outside marriage were institutionalized. But 'fallen women', as they were called, had to endure great prejudices and punishments. Even those who were not sent to the 'madhouse' often had to live a lift apart, marked out as second-class citizens with few rights.

These unmarried mothers formed quite a sizeable group, many of whom were working class. Between Edwardian times and the late 1950s the illegitimacy rate was fairly constant at about 4–5 per cent of all live births (though during the latter years of both world wars the rate almost doubled). This meant that every year there were around 25–35,000 new recruits to this army of the dispossessed. Despite the crusade to improve their condition fought by the National Council for Unmarried Mothers (formed in 1918) most such women remained unaware of each other's existence. They wanted to keep their secret to avoid further discrimination. Around a third of these women, who were usually slightly older, had a common law marriage with the father. They lived together mainly because of the difficulty of getting a divorce at this time. A second smaller group married a few months or years after the birth of their child, perhaps as a result of improved financial circumstances or because the pressure of social convention became too great to defy any longer. Both these groups enjoyed the benefit of mutual support and often did not have to resort to the Poor Law or Public Assistance. The most isolated group were those who maintained little or no contact with the father or who could not marry him. There were perhaps around 10–15,000 women in this position each year, many of them young and desperate. This chapter looks at their experience.

These 'unattached' mothers were seen as the hard core of the social problem of illegitimacy. What circumstances led them to have their illegitimate child? This was a question that was addressed over the years by a host of government committees, Poor Law officials and moral welfare workers. One of the most abiding stereotypes was of the girl who had been led astray as a result of her ignorance and immorality. Even though she may have been seduced by an unscrupulous lover, it was generally thought to be her fault because she allowed her vanity to be flattered and her passions to be inflamed. The language of sin loomed large in the early accounts of the 'fallen woman' but from the 1920s onwards it began to be replaced by a more scientific approach to the 'problem' of the unmarried mother. But beneath the surface of the supposedly scientific theories of the new breed of investigator lay all the old prejudices about the character of the young women 'in trouble'. Doris Odlum's report, 'Unmarried Mothers', appeared just after the Second World War:

There was a powerful and lasting stigma attached to illegitimacy in the inter-war years

The largest number of women who produce illegitimate children are those of inferior mental capacity, especially those whose mentality lies between the range of an intelligence quotient of 65 and 90. The women of this group who produce illegitimate children are frequently emotionally as well as intellectually imma- ture and not only immature but unstable. Their characteristics may be described as falling into two main categories:
(a) those who are deficient in moral and social sense.
(b) those who are too childish to appreciate the moral and social implications of their actions and too lacking in strength of character to stand out against the temptations of the moment.

The life stories of young women who had illegitimate babies enable us to get behind these misleading stereotypes. One important element they missed out was that of sheer chance. It seems to have been not uncommon for a young woman to become pregnant the first time she ever made love to a man. Most of these first-time pregnancies involved 'ordinary lovers' or couples who were just plain unlucky. If there was ignorance involved it was not the educational subnormality suggested in the writings of experts on illegitimacy but rather the lack of sexual knowledge of both partners. Contraception was not widely used amongst young people and whether or not a baby was conceived was very much down to luck. Ada Haskins remembers how she became pregnant in County Durham in 1930 when she was nineteen:

In the mining village, when we were all boys and girls together, we had some beautiful times. And of course I was silly one night. We were out, me and Maggie Tate and her fella and me and Tommy, and he said, you know he had a right wheedling way with women, 'It'll be all right, it'll be all right.' I says, 'I've never been with a man before.' I hadn't, not like that. 'Oh no,' I said, 'it'd scare the wits out of me. I don't know what it's all about.' He says, 'Honestly.' Anyway he wheedled me and wheedled me into it. And in the end I gave way. And I didn't think for one minute that anything could happen the first time you went with a man. I didn't. I hadn't a clue. I was thick as far as sex or anything like that went. We were in a farmer's field, not far from home, because there was fields all around you. That's where they'd all do their courting, the couples, in the fields. I never thought nothing. And Maggie was doing the same, and if it was right for her it was right for me, you know. Because she kept saying, 'Come on, don't be such a spoilsport.' 'But I'm not,' I says, 'I don't think it's right.' I says, 'I'm not married, I'm not even engaged to him, I've only known him seven months.' She says, 'That's all right. Don't worry about it.'

Many other illegitimate births seem to have occurred within courtships where there was an understanding, at least by the woman,

WITH PRESENTATION PORTRAIT OF MRS. GENERAL BOOTH.

THE DELIVERER

LOVE SHALL CONQUER

And Record of Salvation Army Rescue Work.

No. 6.]   LONDON: CHRISTMAS, 1889.   [PRICE ONE PENNY. POST FREE 1s. 6d. PER ANNUM.

In the 1900s Church Army 'sisters' walked the streets at night, handing out posies and propaganda to young women whom they thought were in moral danger

Opposite: Seduction followed by suicide was a popular theme in the early moral welfare literature

that her lover would marry her should she become pregnant. This was not an unreasonable assumption given the fact that 'shotgun weddings' remained common in Britain during the first half of our century. Other circumstances sometimes intervened, however, to make a marriage unsuitable or impossible. The father-to-be might die. This was a very important factor in explaining the rise in illegitimacy during the two world wars. He might lose his job or suddenly hit upon hard times which made marriage and fatherhood a very unattractive prospect. This was probably a much more common cause of illegitimacy in Victorian and Edwardian times than it was later when standards of living were slightly higher and welfare rights were beginning to be extended. He might quite simply change his mind, break the promises he had made and leave his lover to face the consequences by herself. Such allegations were constantly made in young women's efforts to get maintenance payments, or 'affiliation orders' as they were known. Gina Baker, a clerk in London during the First World War, had little doubt that the young officer she was courting would marry her, especially if he got her into trouble. She was later to be proved terribly wrong:

There was a big naval do at Wembley Park and he asked me to bring a friend with me so I took a girlfriend and we went to this do. Well unfortunately, as he was in charge of the spirits, he got drunk. Well I waited thinking to go home with him and it got past twelve o'clock. I was scared to go home because I'd never been home late like that before. And I was frightened. Well, he'd got another friend with him and he said to us 'Come home to my place, the wife's away and you can have the wife's bedroom if you're frightened to go home.' So of course I stayed the night and that was the night I ceased to be a virgin. He was partly drunk and he came into the bedroom because apparently he knew this man and always stayed there. Well he came into the bedroom and of course I was a little bit scared at first, but I liked him and so, of course, trouble was I gave way. And we stayed till the morning and he went back to his bedroom and his friend came and said, 'What did you get up to last night?' 'Course that was all right but I went to the office in the morning and my father came to the office to see where I was, because I hadn't been home all night and it was the first time I'd ever stayed out. And I told a lie and said that I'd been staying with a girlfriend, you see. Of course they found out afterwards that it wasn't true 'cause they saw this girl's parents. There was a terrible to-do and we had a terrific row. Well nothing happened then, but after that it used to become, not once a week, but every time I went out with him. We used to go to his barracks, and go into his room. Then another time he took me to his grandmother and I thought, you know, everything was going to be all right, I'd be able to marry him. And at Christmastime, I stayed at home. It was then that I realized that I was going to have a baby. Well I phoned him and told him and he said, 'Don't worry. I'll see you when I come back.' [He did – but made it clear he had no intention of marrying her.]

Few of those dealing with 'unmarried mothers' – as they came to be known – were prepared to acknowledge the fact that the pregnancy might be the consequence of an unreported rape, either by a lover or perhaps a complete stranger. Life stories reveal that this was by no means uncommon. In 1943 Pat Jones, then just sixteen, lied about her age and joined the WAAF and was stationed at West Kirby near Liverpool. Several months later she was raped:

One night coming off duty an airman stopped me, pushed me to the grass, and that was it. Terrible. I didn't know what to do. I was a virgin. Yes, I was raped. I never saw him before. He was very nasty, not tall but strong. All I remember about him was his nose, quite big. I did not know about contraception. I did not report it because I did not know it would make a baby. It just made me feel very unsafe and I never went back that way again, although it was by the main road in the camp at West Kirby. After three months I

THE ROAD TO RUIN

reported sick. The MO said, 'OK, you can have it and come back into the WAAFs.' I was discharged one month later.

The young women who 'fell' for the married man were often seen as a particularly serious problem by moral welfare workers dealing with illegitimacy. One favoured diagnosis was that she was suffering from a special mental and emotional immaturity. The life stories of the women I have interviewed who bore the illegitimate child of a married man could on one level be read as evidence of this. But more deeply, what they reveal is how many of these women were special victims of the innocent and domestic life that society was preparing them for. Not infrequently, they were middle-class or lower-middle-class women who at home, at school and in their free time had been deprived of informal contact with men. Emily Tucker, the daughter of a Dorset farmer, was sent to a local private girls' school and enjoyed no social life and no boyfriend until the age of twenty-two when she began an affair with an older man who appeared to her to be very sophisticated:

At the office I was working in, I used to go to the bank every day to bank the cash. I used to see this particular bank clerk and we got talking – that's how I met him. And eventually he asked me for a date. He was quite a bit older than me, I should think probably ten years, and this attracted me because I didn't seem to like boys of my own age – they didn't seem to have anything. And as for the farm boys in the village where I lived, I felt I had nothing in common with them at all. This man was different. He was a town man and having come from a remote farm area I felt this was something that suited me so much better – to know a man who wasn't a country boy. He asked me to go out for a drink one night. And he had a car. That was quite an attraction in those days, because not many men had cars, not many young men anyway. And after I'd been out with him once or twice he did tell me that he was married. Well I'd become infatuated by that time and then, of course, the inevitable happened. I found myself to be pregnant.

During the two world wars the atmosphere of uncertainty, separation from loved ones and the ever present possibility of death helped to make this kind of affair much more prevalent. By the later stages of the Second World War adultery in the armed forces had become a great cause for concern – a concern heightened by the fact that many young single women in the WAAF, the Wrens and the ATS worked closely alongside married men, most of them far away from their wives and families. Sometimes an affair with a married man who had a reputation with women was extremely attractive to girls with overbearing or overprotective parents. An affair was – at the time – shocking. It defied sacred family values and it was a passport to a sophisticated adult world denied to them by parents. Monica Fawcett, born in Newcastle in

Rainbow Corner Club in London,
the favourite haunt of American
servicemen and their admirers
during the Second World War.
There was a dramatic increase in
illegitimacy during the war years

Venereal disease became a major health hazard during the Second World War. This poster implicitly attaches blame to the promiscuous woman for the spread of the disease

1927, the daughter of a teacher, had an unhappy relationship with her mother, a devout and rather bigoted Catholic. Her mother had removed her from the local mixed grammar school and sent her to a Catholic convent because she felt 'it was too common'. Monica became pregnant in 1945 at the age of eighteen:

> My brother was on leave from the Navy and he took me down to the Gibraltar Rock in Tynemouth for a drink and to meet one helluva character. This was a lieutenant in the Navy and when I first saw him he was down on all fours barking loudly at a lovely

spaniel dog. I didn't know which appealed to me more, the spaniel or Eric. I thereupon decided that I wanted him to be my sweetheart although as he was almost twice my age and awaiting a divorce from his wife – a thing most uncommon in those days – I didn't think he was entirely of my views. We did however get on very well together and the next day he turned up in his naval uniform to take me out for dinner. My brother then told me that I must forget about him as he was far too old and had a helluva reputation with women. This idea of giving him up did not appeal to me at all; in fact it had completely the reverse effect and made him much more appealing in my view. We had lots of fantastic outings but I still resisted the idea of being immoral. And quite honestly at that time I was totally unaware sexually and it did not appeal to me at all. I looked forward eagerly to each leave and we used to communicate frequently in between. However, after many leaves when I was still on my virtuous behaviour and resisting his advances he went away and I did not receive any letters. I thereupon decided that the next time he came home I was going to let him have his pleasure to the full. I cherished the one letter in which he had declared, 'Yes, I do love you. Eric.' We took up again and one night we were on our own when the air-raid siren sounded and we took shelter in the nearest convenient haystack. All very emotive with the heavy ack-ack guns blasting away and the knowledge that Eric was to be sent overseas. So that was it, although I'm afraid that I was rather a damp squib and told him, 'I didn't like that at all and would much rather have just been kissed.'

Once the baby was conceived the extraordinary innocence and sexual ignorance of some young mothers meant it was often a long time before they realized they were pregnant. Frequently the parents were the first to suspect that a baby was on the way, sometimes because their daughter complained of morning sickness, not realizing it was a symptom of pregnancy. Ada Haskins:

After a couple of months I began to feel terribly sick in the mornings. Because I was so ill, I felt dreadful. So I said to my mother, 'I must have eaten something that's upset me.' She said, 'Why?' I said, 'I'm so sick when I get up in the mornings.' She said, 'What!' Straight away she said, 'Who have you been with?' Straight away. So I said, 'Nobody' at first, 'I don't know what you mean.' She says, 'You've been going out with a fella.' I said, 'Yes I have, Maggie Tate and I have been courting these two fellas.' She said, 'And you've been up to tricks. What did you do?' I says, 'You know what we did. We went together in the field.' She said, 'Oh my God. Right, you'd better get your bags packed and get back to London as quick as you can.' I thought, 'Oh crikey.' I still didn't have a clue what was the matter with me.

Some of those who realized they were pregnant before their parents noticed anything turned to abortion as a way out. It was a way of avoiding an unwanted child and the stigma that could be expected once the pregnancy was discovered. This usually outweighed the fear that it was illegal, punishable by imprisonment, and could be dangerous. The most common method used was the taking of abortifacient pills or medicine. These were made from many different things: traditional herbal remedies like savin or ergot or rye; lead, which was popular in the north and left a tell-tale blue line on the gums; and all sorts of DIY varieties some of which included gunpowder coated in margarine, iron filings, and water in which nails and pennies had been soaked. It was estimated in 1914 that about 100,000 working women took these abortifacients each year. They were often manufactured and sold by quacks, though some women seem to have been genuinely practising a sort of folk medicine. A few of these abortifacients worked, some made the woman ill, while more often they had little or no effect at all. They were advertised in papers as guaranteed to remove 'all female obstructions, irregularities and ailments', and were quite expensive. In Edwardian times they might cost from three to thirty shillings which at the time would be a large slice out of a young woman's weekly wage. They could also be bought locally and in working-class areas information on the shops and homes which stocked them was spread by word of mouth. As well as these quack medicines young women might resort to other traditional remedies like Epsom salts or hot baths or – in desperation – a combination of all of them. Gina Baker:

> He [her lover] gave me a bottle of brown stuff to take to get rid of it. He said, 'That'll take care of it.' Of course I took it home and put it in the drawer and my mother found it. I was so ill because I'd taken all sorts of things. I took two ounces of Epsom salts all at once to get rid of it. And that didn't do any good. On the way home I used to go into the baths and have really hot mustard baths, tried to get rid of it that way but I didn't get rid of it. I'd heard the girls in the office talk about these sorts of things and that was why I tried them. And I was dismissed from the Ministry because I couldn't do my work I was so ill.

When remedies like these failed, as they invariably did, many turned to a backstreet abortionist. Abortion was probably most common in the decades before the First World War when it was widely used – almost as a form of contraception – especially by married working-class women. By the inter-war years the use of condoms and the cap was becoming much more widespread amongst married couples and this new development in birth-control probably reduced the extent of abortions. Nevertheless, in 1937, a government investigation estimated that there were still about 44–60,000 illegal abortions performed each year. It was claimed that a substantial minority of these involved the pregnancies of single women. Girls in trouble might often be told

Although it may not be immediately obvious, this is a turn-of-the-century advertisement for abortifacient pills. There was a terrific demand for pills such as these, yet most had little or no effect at all

76

where they could get an abortion by young friends at work – this was part of the secret knowledge of the shop floor. Sometimes a more experienced boyfriend might suggest where to go. Occasionally, parents might fix an abortion for a young daughter but this practice seems to have been largely confined to the poorer sections of the working class. The abortionists themselves came from all walks of life; there were retired midwives, some of whom did it more for love than money, seeing themselves as providing a necessary social service for the poor; there were surgical stores' owners for whom abortion was often part of the business; and there were unscrupulous quacks and charlatans out to make a fast buck who cared little about their patients.

Betty Brown worked in a jam factory and lived in a poor working-class area of Grimsby in the early 1930s. She remembers some of the horrific techniques used to end unwanted pregnancies:

> My mother used the syringe and carbolic soap. I was very young and frightened when I used to see her go upstairs with hot water in a boiler can. I had seen also the syringe in the bottom drawer. When she had a miss she had a dolly tub in the room and it was full of blood. She was always fainting but she never sent for the doctor. . . . There was no contraception. If you got pregnant you was told by some old woman to go to the chemist and get one shilling's worth of Penny Royal or Bitter Apple and take it with some gin. It used to make you very sick. They used to say keep taking it and you will have a miss. If you was very desperate they used to say use a knitting needle but always have a bottle of Lysol in because of blood poisoning but you died within hours if this happened. Also they used to say soak carbolic soap in hot water and use a syringe. These methods was given us by old midwives, some of them seventy or eighty. . . . One dreadful method we was told by the old midwives was to put the bed mattress at the bottom of the stairs and jump from top to bottom and the shock would cause a miss. My friend died through doing this. Also there was this surgical shop in the town. The man who had it used to sell us boxes of pills. They was like big black bombs, twelve in a box. They cost thirty shillings a box, and after buying three boxes and you didn't have a miss, he used to tell us to go to the back door after tea. And he would use an instrument on you. You always had a miss and terrible flooding would follow. This was all done in secret.

The secrecy with which this whole business was shrouded is indicated by the fact that the police rarely detected more than a hundred abortion offences each year. They were most likely to come to light when something went wrong and serious injury or death followed. Usually the abortion attempt failed and there were few ill effects. But occasional fatal accidents happened when girls tried to abort themselves, usually with anything they had to hand in the home. Knitting needles, crochet hooks and pairs of scissors were often used. The tools and techniques of the backstreet abortionist – especially the most unscrupulous ones – were scarcely more sophisticated. One popular method was to push a stick of slippery elm bark into the womb. Sometimes a syringe would be used to inject an irritant fluid – often a mixture of soap and water – with the aim of inducing an abortion. The descriptions of bloody deaths which resulted from abortion methods like these make gruesome reading. In September 1919, an Edinburgh woman was sentenced to five years in prison for causing the death of a young clerk by performing an illegal abortion:

> There was evidence of considerable loss of blood and the medical witnesses ascribed it to haemorrhage and shock. All the internal organs were healthy and no other condition was found to account for death. The deceased went by arrangement one evening to the house of the prisoner at about five thirty p.m.; she was then in good health and there was no history of previous illness or haemorrhage. She was quite well at nine p.m. except for slight sickness alleged to be due to some strawberries and cream which she had eaten at some time earlier. At nine p.m. deceased went to bed and the prisoner spent a quarter of an hour with her alone. The young woman then became ill, vomited, collapsed and died about eleven p.m. A Higginson's syringe and a basin of water were seen in the room immediately after the prisoner had been with her.

Deaths from the effects of abortions were, however, quite rare. So the young woman, having tried and failed to abort the baby, now had to tell her parents that she was pregnant. Breaking the news was often deeply traumatic for the single girl. A few chose death rather than the disgrace of bearing an illegitimate child. These tragic suicides were always most likely to happen when the pregnant daughter came from a church-going and religious family. A girl from this kind of background was not only breaking a deeply felt family taboo but a religious one as well. Sally Taylor remembers the suicide of her workmate Mary McCarthy in Stepney, East London, in the 1930s:

> Mary McCarthy was a very petite little person. She had long blond hair and wore very high heels. She worked at the Albion knitwear in Cable Street as a machinist. She was much older than me, around nineteen years. Her family was a large one, very poor, but very good Catholics and used to attend St Mary and Michael church in the Commercial Road regularly. On Sunday morning I used to know when she was going to Mass at seven a.m. by the click-clicking of these high heels on the cobble stones. Mary had a young man named Danny Riley, also a good Catholic boy, who played in the Catholic band. He used to look very smart in his uniform, playing the cornet in the Catholic processions that used

to be held in June once a year. Canon Ring was the priest who led all the processions. He ruled his church with a rod of iron and all Catholics went in fear of his wrath. Everyone knew these two were courting and in love but his family was also a large one and all his earnings had to go to his mother who was a widow. The first inkling we all got that all was not well was when Mary kept leaving the machine to run downstairs to the toilet to be sick and we listened to the older women's version of what was wrong with her. As far as I know she kept this secret to herself although everyone had guessed. One day she didn't turn up for work and no one worried about this as they thought she wasn't well again. It must have been about a week later they found her body near Tower Bridge floating in the Thames, her long hair trailing behind her. As the story goes, her young man couldn't marry her. He didn't earn enough to support her and the baby as his own mother needed his money. The disgrace of her condition was too much for her especially as she was a Catholic and you were forbidden sex before marriage. The funeral was a big one, the whole of Cable Street was jam-packed with people. They had to practically carry her young man out to the carriage.

Often young mothers-to-be would conceal their pregnancy for as long as they could. A few managed to hide it to the end, secretly giving birth to their baby in a lone field or locked toilet. Occasionally, through lack of medical care, the mother or baby or both would tragically die. Some planned to abandon or kill the baby, and newspapers of the time sometimes reported the ghoulish discoveries of rotting infant corpses in rivers, quarries and woods. But when the moment for birth came, few could go through with this grisly ordeal. Bertha Williams was a midwife in Bradford during the 1930s:

I once attended a girl and she had been working that day. She'd been to work and she came home from work and was apparently all right. Her mother went out to the pictures as she came in, and her father said he thought she wasn't so well. He said, 'Aren't you so well, love?' And he were a bit suspicious. And he said, 'Is there anything you want to tell me?' She said, 'No.' He says, 'Well, go lie down.' And she went upstairs to lie down, according to him, and eventually she came down and she had the baby in her hands. And she said to him, 'Look what I've got.' He fainted. When he'd pulled himself together he rang for the doctor and the doctor rang me and said, 'Will you come?' because he would never go on his own. . . . Anyway she'd torn the cord, she'd broke the cord. I don't know how she'd done it. She hadn't cut it. She'd just broke it. Either she'd bit it or something, anyway she'd separated it. The baby were bleeding from the cord, she were bleeding, the after-birth was still in her, and to get the baby off it she'd broken it as I say. So the doctor looked, he says, 'Oh, you attend to her, I'll look at the baby.' So eventually we got the afterbirth and we got her cleaned up and tied off the cord and that, but he lived, that baby, he lived in spite of all that. . . . And the girl she was all right and to this day she would never tell anybody who the father was. And her mother coaxed her, she did everything, threatened her, but nobody to this day knows. . . . You see, she'd never told anybody and she had intended to get rid of the baby. She'd bought a new suitcase and in that case was sheets of brown paper and string. And she'd intended to do away with the baby, but once it was born she just couldn't, you see. And she loved that baby so much so that you could hardly take it off her to bath it or do anything with it.

When parents discovered that their daughter was pregnant their first thought was to attack her, either verbally or physically, for the trouble she had brought home. The second was to avoid the shame and stigma of an illegitimate child. The most obvious way to do this was to arrange a marriage if the father-to-be was traceable or thought to be suitable.

Frequently, however, there was no wedding and in homes where there was a troubled relationship between daughter and parents, no thought of arranging one. In these circumstances the young mother-to-be might be told to pack her bags and shown the door. This treatment of pregnant girls was still not uncommon before and during the First World War. After Gina Baker had lost her job secretly trying to abort her baby, her mother realized she was pregnant:

I remember it well; it was a Thursday morning and I went across the road to get a newspaper to see if there was any work going. I came in with the paper and my mother said, 'What do you want a paper for?' I said, 'Well, I want to look for a job.' She said, 'You want to look for another home. Who's responsible?' That's just how she talked. So I hung my head. She said, 'Who is it?' Of course, I had to say it was the naval officer I'd been going out with. 'OK, you take your trouble where you got it from then,' she said. 'You're no longer a daughter of mine. There's the door.' So of course I went to pack some things in a bag. And I'd got a bank book but my mother had taken it and she wouldn't give it to me. All I'd got was ten shillings. And I walked out of that house. My mother stood on that doorstep and she watched me walk up the road.

By the inter-war years harsh attitudes like these were softening a little but many parents were still prepared to carry out the popular threat of sending their pregnant daughter to the workhouse. One important reason for this was that they were just too poor to support her. Most daughters didn't have the money or independence to give them any protection from this kind of parental rejection. Many would be dismissed by their employers, either on moral grounds or because they were thought to be 'unfit for work' as soon as the pregnancy

"*The* GIRL WHO LOST HER CHARACTER"
By Walter Melville

"Take Warning by me,— A Woman without a Character."

became visible. In 1930 Ada Haskins was jilted on the morning of her wedding. Soon afterwards her mother ordered her to return to her job in service in London. Three months later Ada's mistress sent her home again because she could no longer do her domestic duties properly. Ada hoped that her parents would relent and that she could have the baby there:

A publicity picture from a popular Edwardian moral play. A domestic who was pregnant with an illegitimate child would be liable to instant dismissal

> I said, 'I've come home to have the babe.' So she says, 'Well, you can't have it here, you can't stop here.' I says, 'Well, what am I going to do?' She says, 'I don't know, there's only one thing for it. You'll have to go to the workhouse that's all. You can't stop here. I haven't got room for you here.' So my mother had a neighbour, a very nice person and she put me up for a couple of nights then she put me into Roulton House in Chester-le-Street.

Violet Dann's experience was even more tragic. She was brought up in a children's home, then put into service at the age of sixteen. Her master raped her and sent her away to find her parents in Grimsby. She traced her mother who, within a few weeks, died of cancer:

> So I goes looking for my father. I asked somebody if they knew him and they said, 'Oh yes, he lives in Church Street.' So I goes round to my father's and I said, 'Hello, Dad.' Now he recognized me. He said, 'Oh come in, love, have you been home?' and so forth. He said, 'Where are you living now?' and I said, 'I've got

nowhere to go, can you put me up like?' So he looked at the woman he was living with and she said 'Aye, she can come here if she'll go to work.' Anyhow eventually I got a job at the biscuit factory and I were getting bigger and bigger. So she said to me father, 'She's pregnant.' Now, in all my innocence, I knew there was something wrong but I didn't understand babies and that, so I thought I am having a baby. So Father said, 'Whose is it?' But of course he wouldn't believe the story. He says, 'Oh, we can't have that kind of thing here, go on, pack your things and get out. Don't fetch your troubles here.' So eventually I packed my things, I stood on the pavement and I thought well, what am I going to do? Where am I going to go? So I thought the only place I can go to is the workhouse. So I trudged up to the workhouse and they took me in.

In better-off homes parents would also often pack off their pregnant daughters in disgrace. But they wouldn't go to the workhouse – instead they might go to a private nursing home to have the baby in secret. Emily Tucker:

I was terrified to tell my parents. Eventually I told an aunt of mine, my mother's sister, who'd always been very fond of me and very close to me. She must have passed the information on to my mother because the next thing was that I had this summons to come home immediately, which I did. And, of course, I was met with this terrible, terrible atmosphere. 'You've disgraced the family, what have you done, what are you going to do?' And there was many consultations and the man was asked to come and discuss with my parents what should be done. My feelings weren't consulted in any way at all. I had no say in the matter. Because, you see, I wasn't earning enough money to keep myself and a child, and there was no way out – I had to do exactly as my parents told me. And they found a place which they sent me to. It was a nursing home for elderly people in Bournemouth, Boscombe actually, somebody knew somebody who knew somebody. This was how this place was found for me. And I think I was probably about four or five months pregnant. It wasn't noticeable when I went there. And I lived in this place for several months and I think there was an arrangement between my parents and this man to pay for me to be there. And I was there until the child was born. And it was made clear to me all along that this child was going to be adopted. I had no say in the arrangements at all.

Sometimes the pregnant daughter went to stay with relatives in another town and secretly had the baby there. This seems to have been a popular method that families used to avoid the stigma of illegitimacy. Monica Fawcett:

All my family impressed upon me that Eric had been an absolute cad to treat me in this manner and it didn't help me at all that for months we had had no contact. He was a 'married man'. So I was packed off to Lincoln with twelve and sixpence in my pocket and I arrived at my sister-in-law's three-roomed flat where I was met by rather an irate landlord who said that I couldn't stay there. Kathleen was short of money so I first of all took a job in a bicycle factory where I fainted as it was working with machines and I was hopeless at standing for prolonged periods. Then I took a job in a Vim factory where all I did was pull the levers to fill the cans with powder. Here again I fainted. I was meeting with more and more hostility from my sister-in-law's landlord, so I went to the local exchange and asked if they had any residential jobs. There was a barber's shop behind Lincoln Cathedral. The mother was poorly and she had a small boy and a baby to look after so they took me in and I slept with the small boy. They in turn got fed up and said that they couldn't afford to pay me anything. So I went to the public welfare and they decided they would offer me twenty-seven shillings and sixpence. Out of this I paid ten shillings for my board and out of the rest I kept myself and managed to buy a layette for the forthcoming event.

Monica Fawcett in Oxford, 1945

But was the stigma attached to illegitimacy universal amongst British families? Some historians like Peter Laslett have argued it is possible there were some communities in which having children outside marriage was not seen as wrong, and where illegitimacy may have been tolerated or even encouraged. There is some extraordinary statistical evidence which suggests that this may have been the case. These 'deviant' communities were most likely to be rural, because from the mid-nineteenth century onwards, when detailed records began, right up to the 1930s, illegitimacy was generally higher in the countryside than in the towns and cities. This was, in fact, the opposite to other European countries where illegitimacy was considerably higher in the towns. Most interestingly, there were some rural areas where illegitimacy remained consistently high over a long period of time, perhaps suggesting the existence of slightly different sexual and marital customs. For example, Nottinghamshire, the North Riding of Yorkshire and Herefordshire were in the top ten English counties with the highest illegitimacy rates right through from the mid-nineteenth to the mid-twentieth century. And in Scotland, Banffshire was the most prolific county for illegitimacy from the 1850s to the 1930s. That these local patterns of illegitimacy survived the fundamental changes in British society brought about by industrialization and urbanization during the past century and a half is quite astonishing.

Would the pregnant girl in these areas of high illegitimacy be treated any differently? To try to find out I have looked at the remote farming and fishing county of Banffshire in north-east Scotland. During the 1860s its illegitimacy rate had risen to over 16 per cent and even in the early 1920s it was still 12.5 per cent, almost three times the national average in England. The great majority of these unmarried mothers had left home in their teens to work in domestic service on farms or in towns and villages, and they returned to their family home to have their baby. Often the child was looked after by its grandmother, freeing the mother to carry on working. There is little doubt that in late Victorian Banffshire the stigma attached to having a child outside marriage was far less damaging than in most other parts of Britain. In 1886 William Cramond canvassed popular opinion on 'local immorality' for a pamphlet *Illegitimacy in Banffshire*. These are some typical comments he collected:

> A bank official: I have heard many a mother of this kind say, 'It's nae sae bad as stealing, or deein' awa' wi' the puir craters.'
> A clergyman: A mother excuses her fallen daughter by saying, 'Puir thing, it's a misfortune, but she'll get ower it.' And the neighbours chime in and add, 'It wad hae been waur if she had ta'en anything.'

To discover how far these traditional attitudes survived into the twentieth century I have tried to tap living memory in Banffshire today. My interviews suggest that they did not survive for long. By the

85

inter-war years unmarried mothers and their children in this area were beginning to form an outcast group of the very poor who were ashamed of their inferior social status and who were subjected to considerable hostility and discrimination. Interestingly, this corresponds to some extent with the gradual decline in illegitimacy in Banffshire which, especially from the late 1930s onwards, began to conform more closely to the national average. This change perhaps had something to do with the gradual loosening of old kinship networks with the move to the towns, the decline in the importance of domestic service and the quest for a higher standard of living. In the 1920s and 1930s it is clear that the experience of illegitimacy was as harsh and painful in Banffshire as anywhere else in Britain. Betty Stokes was the illegitimate daughter of a gamekeeper born in 1912 who was brought up in a Banffshire village with her brother and sister – also both illegitimate – by her mother and grandmother. They all lived in a tiny one-roomed croft house with no running water or sanitation. Her mother, who was the breadwinner, left at six o'clock each morning to walk three miles to work in farm service, rarely returning until half-past eight in the evening.

Children can be cruel and words can be vicious weapons. I well remember the word 'bastard' being shouted at me in the play-ground. It was a constant reminder of what I was. The teachers as well, they often didn't help. They were local and knew about me. I was sorted out from my early days at school and put in the front seat. I sat alongside four other illegitimate children that were in my class. But for me, personally, this was a good thing. We were equal. Going through school was difficult; friends could not be made easily because we were different. The other children talked about their fathers, they were very important to them, and we felt left out. But among ourselves we could talk, and the question of father never came into it. But you were singled out. If the minister's daughter or the doctor's daughter was in class the teacher would not allow us to sit with them. It bothered me a lot. I felt withdrawn and I could not take part in the normal things. I was in tears a lot and very often I played truant because of it. But there was no escape because it was a small community and people rarely moved away so everyone knew about us. I remember a lady had a baker's shop and we used to buy bread there. I was sent across the road to get a loaf. But we did not have any money to pay for it and she said, 'Of course, your father won't have paid for you yet.' He paid about a pound a month, and it was such a degrading expression, it really hurt me. I know it affected me so much that I made up my mind never to get married and never to have a family, I resented my situation so much. I did get married and have children in the end but I never told my husband's parents that I was illegitimate and when I filled out the wedding certificate I created a father for myself so that they wouldn't know.

The 'unmarried' working-class mother and her child must have had a bleak and difficult time – wherever they lived. But those who could count on their family for support probably enjoyed more dignity and freedom than those who had to look to the Poor Law or the church for help, especially when the baby was about to be born. When family failed to provide for a pregnant daughter a sinister band of institutions beckoned her. The most infamous and dreaded of all was, of course, the workhouse. The treatment of 'unmarried mothers' in workhouses had changed little since the 1830s when, under the new Poor Law, a policy emphasizing the stigma of bastardy had been pursued. This was achieved by refusing most single pregnant girls outdoor relief and subjecting them to a harsh punitive regime once they were inside the workhouse. The grim heyday of the workhouse as the last refuge of the unmarried mother was in late Victorian times but even in the Edwardian era it was still dealing with about one in five of all illegitimate births. And even though the workhouse was officially abolished in 1929 – to be replaced by Public Assistance institutions – it continued much as before in all but name, using the same buildings and practices right up until the coming of the welfare state after the Second World War.

In addition to the workhouse, there was a cluster of church-run homes for 'unmarried mothers' whose spartan and punitive regimes were very similar. Although their purpose was not to deter – like the workhouse – but to reform the character of the fallen girl, and instil in her values of duty and discipline, this reformatory purpose was modelled on early prisons, and it sometimes led to even greater severity. These institutions had a variety of names – reformatories, penitentiaries, refuges, maternity homes and Mother-and-Baby homes were the most common. The Social Purity and Hygiene Movement and Evangelical groups like the Church Army and the Salvation Army were amongst the pioneers of this provision.

What was it like for the young women who became the reluctant guests of the workhouse, or the church-run home or reformatory for 'unmarried mothers'? First of all, like prisoners, they lost all personal rights, freedom and privacy. Their mail was censored and only a few liberal homes allowed an inmate to open her own mail – and even then the matron would be present to remove it quickly if she found it unsuitable or offensive. After being turned out on the streets, Gina Baker entered a Church Army home in Brighton in 1918:

> Well, these homes for Wayward Girls were, I tell you, more or less prisons. You were treated just as if you were a prisoner. You wasn't allowed money, you wasn't allowed writing paper, you wasn't allowed anything. And the meals were really atrocious. They were very, very strict. You wasn't allowed to do this, you wasn't allowed to do that. You had work to do and you worked hard. You worked scrubbing and cleaning and washing. They said that the working did you good.

Often the girls' own clothes were removed in exchange for a drab uniform. Ada Haskins:

> Your clothes were taken away from you. You were given a horrible grey dress and a coarse apron, an apron made from an old sack. And your stockings was taken away from you. You wore a pair of old heavy clogs. Oh my God, my ankles within a week were chaffed red raw.

Every day was organized into a series of closely supervised tasks which were enforced with relentless discipline. The aim was to crush the former character of the inmate and replace it with a conformist one. In 1919, F. J. Wakefield described the regimented daily round of the penitentiary for fallen girls in *Rescue Work: An Enquiry and Criticism*:

> On entering the house that is to be her home for two or three years the girl steps into a life that is ordered with clockwork precision; every minute has its appointed task, or set recreation, or time of devotion. To an undisciplined girl who has known neither silence

A Church Army home for young 'unmarried mothers' in the early 1920s. Most of these unfortunate young women were issued with a cap and apron and trained for a life as a domestic, whether they liked it or not

nor method these ordered days of work and devotion are apt to be trying; some get restless or insubordinate, and run away or are sent away; but the majority fall into the daily routine and if there is an atmosphere of love in the home, grow quieter and happier under the gentle pressure of constant supervision and regular work, and when the time comes to leave may even weep and beg to stay. 'The first few months are difficult for them,' said a nun, 'but after that they nearly all settle down.'

The great aim of this system of training is to ensure that old things shall be forgotten and newness of life taught in every possible way. In most penitentiaries the girls 'never go outside the garden of the home', for 'it unsettles them to go out', and 'they are never left alone in each other's company day or night; so no loophole of opportunity is given for those evil communications which tend to blight the beginnings of good.'

The routine of a typical working day was as follows:

All rise at 6.15 and are in chapel at 6.50; breakfast is at 7.10, then all make their beds and tidy their cubicles. At 7.45 they separate for work, some to the wash-house and laundry and some to the house and kitchen. Silence is observed at work. They are changed occasionally from one kind of work to another, as seems best for training them for what they wish to be. Some learn to be general servants or kitchen maids, but most learn laundry work. At 10 o'clock they sit down for rest and lunch, work again till 1 o'clock, when they stop for dinner and recreation. At 2 o'clock the girls go back to work and the house girls now sit in the classroom with the sister, mending and making clothes and knitting stockings. At 5 o'clock comes tea time, then a second recreation, from 6 to 8 there is work again; then comes the third recreation time spent in reading or in scripture class. They separate at 8.30, and then all go to chapel as in the morning. At 9.20 all go to bed.

The daily routine of workhouses was often quite similar to this and they often demoralized the young inmates. Violet Dann entered the Grimsby workhouse in 1932:

I went working in the laundry there. They had all these bare brick walls and the bottom was dark green paint and yellow paint and great big long tables and forms that used to be scrubbed. It was just like a back yard with a roof put on top. It was very dismal and dull and it was horrible. At that time I felt very bitter and lost. I got to the point of not caring whether I lived, died, survived or what happened. I was so low in spirits. I stopped eating because I was fretting. The doctor saw me and said, 'She's killing herself with fretting.'

The work the young women did was domestic labour, mostly laundry work, housework, and needlework. This employment was often essential to the very survival of these institutions. They were usually desperately short of funds and 'fallen' inmates provided a free labour supply which meant they could be run on a shoestring. Their work – especially taking in laundry from outside – also provided them with their main source of income. The discipline and drudgery of domestic labour was in any case seen as good training – or for some a penance – for young fallen women. On leaving the institution they would then be conveniently found jobs as domestics in the homes of local middle-class families who would provide close moral supervision for them in the future. So whatever the background or occupation a girl came from, and whatever her stage of pregnancy, she would quickly be issued with a washtub, a broom and a needle and told to get on with it. Even former domestics used to this kind of arduous labour found themselves close to breaking point, especially when they were near to giving birth as was Ada Stupple:

> My God, I wouldn't wish them on my worst enemy, places like that. There were stone floors, cobbles, brick floors and white wooden tables, that had to be scrubbed every day. . . .They used to say 'Get on with your work, get on with your work,' that's all they used to say to you. You were given so much to do; some days I don't know at the end of the day how I stood up. It was dreadful. There was scrubbing the tables, scrubbing all the stone floors, all the loos, cleaning the wards out, because they had sick people there, old people, sick, babies being born, you used to have to do all the hard work right until your time was ready. Work like a horse, a horse couldn't have worked any harder. And dragging pails of water, hot soda water, great big scrubbing brush, it was dreadful. It was really heart-breaking. You were there as workers, that's how you were tret. And you were allowed to go to bed at nine o'clock and you had to be up at half past four. And you worked from half past four in the morning. You got a slice of bread and a mug of tea. There was never a breakfast of any sort, always bread and dripping or bread and jam, bread and marmalade.

Regular religious instruction, attendance at daily chapel and Sunday services were a very important part of church-run institutions for young fallen women. Violet Dann was transferred to a Salvation Army Home in Newcastle where she had to take part in daily prayers for forgiveness – even though she had told the sister she had been raped.

> You went down and you knelt down and you asked for forgiveness for what you'd done. I knelt down and asked for forgiveness but it wasn't because of what I'd done. I just asked for forgiveness for the things that had happened to me.

Some rebelled against the tyranny of these regimes but the odds were stacked against any resistance. The young inmates had ended up there because they had nowhere else to go, and if they were in the later

Before and after training for service. These Church Army publicity pictures of the 1930s illustrate its aim of transforming the 'fallen' young woman of the period into an obedient and dutiful domestic

stages of pregnancy they would not want to risk being turned out on the streets again – which was the ultimate sanction of these institutions. Even minor acts of defiance seem to have been classed as 'insubordination', the penalty for which was expulsion. Gina Baker had sought refuge with the Church Army who had dispatched her to one of their 'homes' in Brighton. She describes the circumstances in which she was expelled from this institution:

> I was there for a little while, not long, and I thought 'Well, why can't I write to the man responsible.' But she wouldn't give me the paper so I got a bit of toilet paper and I wrote on the toilet paper and pinched an envelope, put it in the envelope, but I hadn't got any money for a stamp. So as we came out to go to church – they used to march you along the street to church – the man at the gate, a kind of gardener, I said to him, 'Will you post this letter for me please? I haven't any money for a stamp.' I gave it to him and when we came back from church the matron sent for me and she said, 'Is this your writing?' He'd taken it straight back to the home and given it to the matron. I said, 'Yes,' and she said, 'How dare you. I can have you summonsed for stealing. You stole that envelope and that paper.' I said, 'It's only toilet paper.' 'It makes no difference,' she said. 'I'm sorry, you can't stop here; you'll have to go back to London.' So back to London I had to go without any dinner. They put me on the train there and then.

Most of the young women who peopled these harsh institutions came from a working-class background. Better-off parents with a pregnant daughter would often send her to a private nursing home where the treatment was very different, as Emily Tucker discovered when she arrived at the home in Bournemouth in the early 1930s:

> It was a lovely big comfortable house. Once I was away from home I was treated all right, because they didn't treat me as if I was an outcast. They were paid and I suppose that suited them. But I certainly wasn't treated badly by them at all.

What became of all these 'unmarried mothers' and their children? To begin with because of the difficult circumstances they often found themselves in, the mothers and their new babies had a much greater chance of dying in childbirth. Around the time of the First World War it was statistically twice that of those who were married. Those babies who survived would often be brought up by their young mother's parents, a married sister, an aunt or other relative. Often they imagined these were their real parents and were only told the truth – if at all – many years later. The mother would hand over most of her wages to whoever was bringing up her child. Parents often put great pressure on their daughter to arrange the child's upbringing in this way for it provided a way of passing off the child as legitimate and sometimes the payment of this 'maintenance money' was much sought after.

Some mothers battled – as far as they could – to bring up their child themselves, but it was a hard road. The mother's employment opportunities and income were greatly reduced because she had to look after her child, or pay for a child minder, or arrange for it to be boarded out with a foster mother. The mother rarely received any maintenance money to help with this. Although affiliation orders were established in law they were very easy to avoid, not least because there were no officials appointed to collect the money. During the inter-war years only one in five unmarried mothers received maintenance money. Some chose adoption – or had it chosen for them by their parents or by the institution they were in. They were normally not told by the adoption agency where the baby had gone and consequently lost touch with their child, often a source of great regret in later life. The most unfortunate of all were perhaps those who, for a variety of reasons, stayed in the workhouse for several months or years, or who were classified as being 'moral imbeciles' or 'feeble-minded'. They often found that their children were taken away from them and placed in childrens' homes or reformatories on the grounds that they were hereditarily tainted with the ignorance and immorality of their parents.

For most, the early months and years of motherhood were probably a desperately unhappy time. Many must have at least toyed with the idea of suicide as the only way out. In 1919 Gina Baker was thrown out on to the streets after an argument with her sister who had been sheltering her and her new baby.

Gina Baker cuddles her baby shortly after she tried to drown herself and her illegitimate child

I walked out with the baby – no clothes for myself, and only a nappy for the baby I rolled in a shawl. I was coming over the bridge by the canal, and I thought, 'What can I do? Life isn't worth living.' And so I went down the steps to go and drown myself. And a man came down after me, got hold of me and he said 'oh no you don't!' He said, 'I've got daughters of my own. What's the trouble?' And I said, 'You leave me alone!' When I turned round he said, 'Good God! You're George's daughter!' So I said, 'What's that to you?' He said, 'Come on, I'm taking you home.' And it was through him that I went to the front door to knock, and when I knocked at the door my father opened it and he said, 'We expected you, come in,' and they took me in. And my mother said, 'You've come home then.' And I was crying. She said, 'You'd better go to your room; it's where you left it.' She said, 'I'll see you in the morning.'

In most people's eyes these young women – whatever their fate – were not to be pitied too much. They had broken the rules and had to pay the price. Their misery and unhappiness was held up before the young as an example of the dreadful consequences of defying authority. Daughters were constantly reminded that if they brought 'trouble' home they would be sent to the workhouse. The reality was horrific enough but fact became mixed with fiction to create a folklore of fear. Some young people were convinced that 'bad girls' were rolled up in carpets and suffocated; some believed they could be deported for bearing a 'bastard' child; and others thought that young unmarried mothers and their babies were frequently drowned in the dead of night. As a result, sex before marriage became tinged with terror. Many young women had at the back of their minds the fear that one taste of the forbidden fruit could ruin their life. It was a short road to the workhouse and the madhouse.

4

COURTSHIP RITUALS

In 1936 Gwen Taylor, then seventeen, went to stay with her parents in the village of Kempshot, near Basingstoke, during some leave from her job as a nursemaid. The young man she was courting, an electrician, later to become her husband, was also a guest in the house. One evening they went out for a walk into the country together and made love for the first time:

> I took a lot of persuading, because it was my upbringing, but he'd already asked me to marry him and get engaged, so I thought, 'Oh well, he'll wonder why I'm stalling,' so that was it. But it was very difficult going home that night. It was awkward because my father always looked you up and down very closely when you walked in the house, to see if you looked guilty, and I had a job not looking guilty. . . .Where it happened was near my home, round one of the country lanes. I didn't feel very happy about it. I felt that I'd been too easy, to be quite frank; it was the way we were brought up then. We were brought up to think it was wrong in those days. With most of the girls I knew it was because 'Oh, this is the man,' you know, and I think in lots of cases they felt they had to please them or they'd look elsewhere. And I think that was a lot of the trouble.

Gwen Taylor's first experience of sex was far from being a passionate or pleasurable event. She agreed to it in order to please and hold on to her husband-to-be. The most powerful feeling she associates with it are guilt and fear of detection. Her experience was probably fairly typical of most of the women who entered into what was an illicit sexual relationship with their fiancé or lover between the 1890s and the 1950s. For during this period courtship involved the observance of a ritual of female chastity and innocence. Sex before marriage between courting couples was probably more taboo than at any other time in modern British history.

Although values of chastity and sexual restraint were nothing new, in previous centuries a blind eye had often been turned to sexual contact between young men and women who intended to marry. But under the influence of Victorian sexual taboos, the first half of our century was to be a period of intense sexual self-restraint and sexual guilt among very young people who were 'going steady'. Nevertheless, sex did not disappear altogether from courting relationships. Rather, lovers who did have sex went to extraordinary lengths to keep it a private affair.

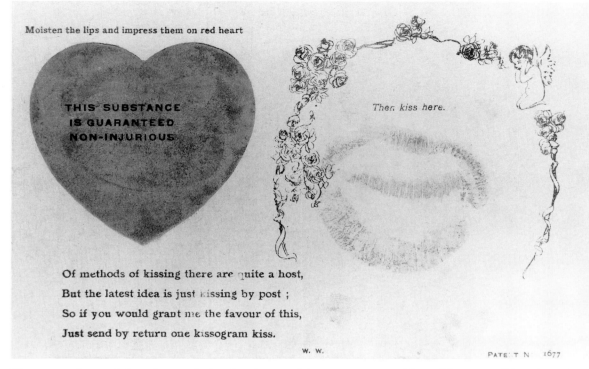

Moisten the lips and impress them on red heart

THIS SUBSTANCE
IS GUARANTEED
NON-INJURIOUS

Then kiss here.

Of methods of kissing there are quite a host,

But the latest idea is just kissing by post ;

So if you would grant me the favour of this,

Just send by return one kissogram kiss.

W. W.

PATENT N 1677

A kissogram, Edwardian style. These cards were often sent by secret admirers or courting couples. This one was posted in Gateshead in 1906

However, the social and sexual rituals of courtship were very unfair. They were heavily weighted in favour of men and more often than not disadvantaged and discriminated against women. This chapter tells the story of these rituals and the secret world in which they were practised and broken.

Between the last years of Queen Victoria's reign and the 'never-had-it-so-good' days of the late 1950s, courtship took on a new ritualistic and much more formal appearance in Britain. Its main features were a lengthy period of engagement or serious courting, a strong disapproval of sex before marriage and a high age of marriage. During the Edwardian period the average age of marriage was higher than at any other moment in British history, peaking at twenty-seven years for men and twenty-six for women. It remained high in the 1930s with an average of twenty-six for men and twenty-four for women, and only dropped significantly in the 1950s. Perhaps most spectacular of all, though, was an increasingly elaborate marriage ceremony which celebrated the virgin bride. These rituals were in part a reflection of the power of adults over youth during this period. This was a time when at school, at work and in leisure hours young people from all social classes enjoyed few rights and were often strictly controlled by adults. The rituals were also the product of a new sexual conformity and uniformity across much of Britain. In the industrial age the massive growth of state bureaucracy, compulsory schooling and the growth of the popular press were all powerful vehicles for conformity, crushing many of the informal and (to most middle-class Victorians) immoral sexual customs which had originated in the countryside. Common law marriage or 'living tally' as it was known; 'besom' weddings, a secular right that allowed self-marriage and self-divorce; bundling and night visiting where courting couples slept together before marriage; and the old rural tradition of pre-bridal pregnancy, a test of fertility; all these traditions and others, quite common among the poorer classes, were by the beginning of the twentieth century little more than memories in most areas. By Edwardian times, values of sexual purity and sexual respectability, championed by the church, the state and the middle classes had penetrated all but the very lowest and very highest echelons of society. These values became enshrined in an ideal of a chaste courtship, leading to a white wedding for the virgin bride, that was to remain ascendant until the late 1950s.

Memories of courting days illustrate just how powerful adults used to be in shaping young people's lives. Their influence and control often restricted or prevented altogether a sexual relationship developing between courting couples. Most of the control was exercised by parents. Although young people initially chose partners for themselves, it was generally accepted that parents should have some say in whether their choice was a suitable one; where the couple went; what they did together; what time they should arrive home; whether or not they should get engaged and when they should be married. In the late Victorian and Edwardian years it was a big say, especially when young people under twenty-one were involved, for they needed parental permission to marry. Control had relaxed a little by the 1950s but courtship during the period as a whole was characterized by a high degree of ritualized parental intervention and interference. Parents set the agenda for courting and it was a formal and moralistic one which often left little or no room for sexual experience.

The regulation of the courtship often began from its inception. Well-to-do parents would carefully select guests for parties and dances with a view to their son or daughter choosing an eligible partner. Respectable parents with less means would encourage their children to go to the 'right' places like social clubs attached to the local church or chapel with the same end in sight. They were by no means always successful in influencing their choices, especially among the working classes where the street, the park, the monkey parade, the cinema and the youth club were the most common places where courtships began, usually as a result of a chance encounter. Nevertheless, even when a girlfriend or boyfriend was found independently – as was often the case – there were two rituals of introduction to the parents which usually gave them the opportunity to vet the prospective partner and to establish some sort of moral supervision and control over any courtship that might develop.

First was the ritual request for permission from the girl's parents

before taking her out for the evening. Among the respectable working class this often involved knocking on the parents' door and introducing yourself. Among the middle classes it was usually a more formal business and the old Victorian convention of writing to ask the father's permission was still alive and well before the First World War. Grace Sykes, the daughter of an actuary born in 1889, remembers how at the age of sixteen, she came to go out with her husband-to-be after meeting him in a London park:

> He ended up by asking me if I'd go out with him to a musical on the Saturday. Well I was never allowed out after half-past eight at that time. So I said to him, 'Good gracious, no.' He said, 'Not the first house?' Because there used to be two houses from seven till nine and then from nine till eleven. So I said, 'Good gracious, no. My father would have a fit if I asked.' Do you know what he did? He wrote to my father. I thought I was in for a good old wigging. Dad came down to breakfast one morning and he said, 'Grace, I want to speak to you in the study.' I wondered what on earth I'd done. Into his study I went, and he said, 'I've had a letter from a young gentleman called Hargrave.' So I thought, what a cheek, what is he writing to you about? He said, 'When a gentleman approaches me in a gentlemanly manner I treat him as a gentleman.' And apparently he'd written to ask Dad if he could take me out to the Music Hall, to the first house in the evening. And I said, 'Can I go?' So surprised. He said, 'Yes. I've told your mother to answer it, providing he fetches you and brings you home.'

By the inter-war years this kind of formality was seen as very old-fashioned and was often dispensed with. Some couples might, without fear of displeasing their parents, go out with each other several times as long as they did not shirk the second and more important ritual introduction to the parents, usually over Sunday tea. The venue would normally be the daughter's family home. All the best china would be on display and the suitor would wear his smartest clothes. He would be very much on his best behaviour. This introduction could be nerve-racking for the young man, for the whole purpose of the ritual was for her parents to assess his suitability. Character, class background, status, religion, age, appearance and occupation would all be vetted. If he didn't pass the test – and many didn't – the parents would put strong pressure on the daughter to finish the relationship. Even in slum areas these rituals were often observed. Ray Rochford remembers them from his courting days in Salford near Manchester in the late 1930s:

> After you'd seen a girl for a few weeks her mother would want to know who her daughter was seeing, so you got invited home for tea, usually on a Sunday, in the front room. The front room was like a mausoleum, you see; it was only used for weddings and funerals; nobody went in there, that was sacrosanct. And she'd

This Edwardian comic postcard plays on the tension between courting couples and parents over evening curfews

ask you, 'Come home for tea on Sunday.' Well, you knew what that meant, that was a danger sign. After you'd been to tea you were walking out with a girl, then you might get engaged and wedding bells was in the air. But I liked this girl; Ailif Jones, her name was. I liked her a lot, so naturally I went there, and knocked on the door at seven o'clock. 'Come in, front room on the left.' Not in the kitchen near the fire. And her father was there and her mother. He was a collector for the Prudential. I'll always remember him with his bowler hat and little moustache, long black mac, bike clips round his trousers and a big black bike. And he used to go around collecting twopences and threepences. His job wasn't that great; he was probably only earning about two pounds ten a week but he had the white collar and tie on you see, so he wasn't working class. People used to delude themselves they wasn't working class. And he was a Methodist lay preacher, he used to rant and rave on Sundays. Well, half-way through the tea he asked 'Where do you work?' 'I work in a mill in Ordsall Lane.'

'Asking Papa.' A suitor asks the father's permission to marry his daughter. This ritual was still widely practised in Edwardian times – evidence of much greater parental power then than now

'Well, what's your job?' 'Bobbin lad.' That was just collecting bobbins out of a machine, that was a menial job. 'What school did you go to?' 'All Souls,' that was Catholic, oh that was another stroke against me, right away you see, with him being a Welsh Methodist and Catholics having idols and all that popery. He wasn't having his daughter going out with a Catholic, a left-footer as they called them in those days. So I blew my chances with answering those two questions. And then he just retired behind his newspaper and that was it. As far as he was concerned I was a non-runner. And I could see her looking at her mother and her mother looking at her, and of course at the end of the tea we went out and she said, 'I don't know when I'll see you again.' You get the message, you see. And as far as she was concerned, that was over, that was the end of the relationship. What her parents said went for her, you see. She was only sixteen and she wouldn't go against her parents by going out with a Cross Lane ike.

If the test was passed, this formal ritual left the couple in little doubt – if they had any before – that they had a strong moral responsibility to uphold the family's respectability and good name. From this point onwards they were said to be 'keeping company' or 'walking out together'. Parental supervision would be maintained in occasional ritual meals, often at both sets of parents. If there was any sniff of illicit sex the couple ran the risk of stirring up serious parental disapproval which might endanger the future of the courtship. While courting, many young men took great pains to create a respectable image and they would often give up – at least temporarily – some of their old friends and more dubious habits like heavy drinking, and become particularly chivalrous and considerate. Many parents were keen to oversee these budding relationships but since most young people – especially from the working classes – chose marriage partners from within their own communities formal supervision was often unnecessary. It was not difficult to monitor their activities through neighbours and local gossip. In working-class areas the local mothers who met regularly on the streets, in corner shops and in pubs were often one step ahead of the young lovers. Budding courtships were high on the list of local gossip. This was because they touched on key concerns of the working-class community like family pride, the fear of illegitimacy and economic well-being or survival. In many families the parents' efforts to control the courtship and delay the marriage of their sons and daughters – especially daughters – was born out of economic necessity or a desire to maintain a slightly higher standard of living. Valuable breadwinners were lost when children married and this economic value was especially important in single parent families. Considerations like these, of which young people were acutely aware, often reinforced adult control over courtship by inextricably tying it up with loyalty and care for the well-being of the parents.

A courting couple pose beside their Chevrolet car in 1926. Many a middle-class courtship was consummated in the back of a motor car

Young people who left home in their teens to continue their education or to find employment sometimes enjoyed little or no more freedom to consummate a serious relationship than those who stayed behind. Employers and educational or training institutions took their duties of moral control of the young very seriously – especially the control of young women. Most working-class girls left home to enter domestic service, take up nursing or some shop work, which were often characterized by 'living in' arrangements. There would usually be fairly strict rules governing what girls could and could not do in their few spare hours each week. Evening curfews were enforced, usually at nine o'clock, just as they would have been at home. There were sex segregated sleeping arrangements. Sometimes suitors or 'followers', as they were called, were barred. And if there was a hint of sexual disobedience employers might write to a girl's parents or threaten her with dismissal without a character, which would seriously damage her employment prospects. Young women who entered teacher training colleges fared little better. Annie Ford attended Stockwell teacher training college just before the First World War:

> Eight o'clock, I think, was the latest we were in and if you didn't get in until eight you had to sign where you were going to have tea. And when you went up to college your parents had to send a list of the people whose homes you might visit, if there were any – to go and stay for the fortnightly weekend you see – and the visitors you

might have come to see you in college. And no man was ever allowed through, except a clergyman. It was a very strict life, very strict. Sundays, we had to go to service morning and evening unless you got excused. If there was any reason for not going you had to go to the matron and be excused. And on Monday mornings slips of paper were handed round to everybody and you'd to say which church you'd been to and what text the sermon was preached from.

The ritual of courtship then was one in which strict adult control greatly restricted the opportunities for sex before marriage. Some young people simply accepted this ritual and the values it enshrined, and seem to have had little or no desire to taste the forbidden fruit. They had other things on their minds. Most important of all was often the home that they would be moving into when they were married. The postponement of marriage in the first half of our century was in part testimony to the increasing ambition of couples to start married life in a comfortable home of their own – rented if they were working class, or privately owned with the help of a mortgage, for the better-off. Courtship was a time of relentless saving for a mortgage, for a favourite three-piece suite or, more humbly, for the 'bottom drawer', and this saving ethic probably passed, perhaps subconsciously, into the realm of sex. Couples 'giving in' to sexual desire, in an age when contraception and abortion were not freely available, were taking quite a big risk. An unwanted pregnancy and the family disgrace that would probably follow in its wake, could ruin a couple's careful plans for wedded bliss. Couples were controlling and reducing the number of children they had much more, primarily so that they could enjoy a higher standard of living. This trend had begun in late Victorian times and by the 1930s large families of more than five children were only characteristic of the lower levels of the working class. To achieve the goal of the small family required restraint both before and after marriage.

In many courtships, however, a powerful brew of social pressures and sexual passions brought lots of couples close to illicit sex. This was where some of the unwritten rules of the courtship ritual really came into play. These rules seem to have sprung from the age-old tradition of the double standard. Most girls were taught by their mothers that – as Lil Trufit, a domestic servant in London before the First World War, put it – 'It is the boy's place to ask, and the girl's place to refuse, because no man wants to marry a girl who gives in to anybody.' Because most warnings against sexual misconduct were directed at young women, and because they had most to lose from an unwanted pregnancy, many took this advice to heart. They rarely seem to have initiated sex. It was usually left to the young man to make the sexual advance, and as often as not it would be rebuffed and the relationship would remain platonic until the marriage. Rose Sherwin was born in Hanley, Staffordshire, in 1895:

I brought my boy home on my nineteenth birthday at my parents'
request. Dad wanted to size this young man up and tell him what
sort of a girl he was courting and what would happen to him if
anything happened to me. I told Dad that nothing would happen
to me as Joe was having boxing lessons at the Boys' Brigade at his
chapel. We were both good Methodists. After the birthday I was
allowed to go to Chapel with Joe one Sunday and he came to our
Chapel on alternate Sundays. Well, by this time the First War was
on and Joe enlisted in the Royal Field Artillery. The night before
he went we went for a long walk and we stopped for a cuddle
against some railings around a field. He tried to put his hand
down my blouse at the front so he got a slap across his face as he
did. So after that our courting was letter writing and short leaves
every three months. He tried several times to do what I felt was
very wrong but never succeeded. I told him I thought he was a
Christian like me and I kept my body clean. We got engaged when
I was twenty and married on my twenty-first birthday. I still had to
be in the house by ten o'clock even after I married. On my
wedding night I said to my dad, 'How am I going to get undressed
with Joe in the bedroom?' Dad agreed to keep him in conversation
until I was in bed so I went upstairs and was in bed by the time he
came up. Well, it happened, of course, but I told him I didn't
know what he had done.

The major British sex surveys strongly indicate that the proportion
of those who had sex before marriage was gradually increasing from
the 1900s onwards. This supports the claims of moral reformers of the
time who argued that more courting couples were having sex in the
1930s than before the First World War. Many gloom and doom reports
claimed that this 'moral decline' was greatest among the middle classes
and that it was directly related – more than anything else – to car
ownership amongst the young. Though unintended by the inventors,
the new roofed-in models that were mass-produced from the 1920s
onwards were certainly well suited to the needs of couples eager for
sexual experience. They were snug, dark 'boxes' that could be driven
daringly fast, to remote lanes many miles from the watchful eyes of
parents and neighbours. Popular newspapers often portrayed them as a
menace to morality and there is little doubt that many courtships and
affairs were consummated in the back of a Ford 8 or an Austin 7 after
an evening in a country pub. However, these reports and surveys tell us
little or nothing about the thoughts and feelings that lay behind sex
before marriage and what it meant to courting couples. To begin to
answer questions like these we have to turn to living memory.

What emerges most powerfully from people's memories is that
despite a slight relaxation in sexual taboos the closer you get to the
present, sex before marriage among courting couples was a minefield
of guilt, anxiety and fear. These emotions seem to have deeply afflicted

Front cover of a popular women's magazine in 1936. It vividly illustrates the pressures for social and sexual conformity during this period

many women. What emerges from their stories is a secret world of sex in back streets, fields and parents' living-rooms.

Emily McNulty remembers her first sexual experiences with her husband-to-be in Accrington, Lancashire, in the early 1920s. 'I was nervous when we made love because my dad's voice always came to me: "Don't come home if you get into trouble."' This anxiety was heightened by the fact that there was rarely a private space to make love: it was fast and furtive and there was a constant fear of detection. Pat Dyer, a cleaner, was courting in Barnsley, Yorkshire, around the same time. 'We started having sex when I was seventeen but I hated it. It was a quick affair standing in doorways or dark alleys in winter and we went for walks in summer in fields or a wood.'

If a young woman appeared to be too keen for sex before marriage, or if she agreed to sex too easily, even at all, then she might seriously damage her marriage prospects. The man was generally thought to have strong sexual urges and if he failed to contain them as was only 'natural' from time to time, it was the duty of the young woman to resist. For if she was 'good' she was assumed to be much more sexually pure and passive. An attempt to have sex with a girlfriend quite early on in a relationship was in some ways a test to see if she was a 'good' girl likely to make a loyal and obedient wife. Many girls learned through bitter experience that to succumb too soon to sex invited rejection as a potential wife and a 'bad' reputation among the young men. John Binns remembers this cynical approach towards young women:

> When you got the right girl you decided that no matter how hard you tried you would never get sex and that was a good thing. And then you realized that it's not an easy thing sex; you shouldn't treat it as a light thing. You know that you'd got a good girl then, a girl that would never give in; you knew that she was good. It was a terrible thing, but if she gave away things pretty easy you went out for a certain time, whether you got fed up with her or not, but you ditched her and went with someone else. So the more easy she was the less chance she'd got of hooking a man or getting married to a man. It was ridiculous really but that's how it was. I think you looked down on them when they were too easy, when they let you have it too often and I suppose it's like good food, you can have too much of it and you can get fed up with it, it's as simple as that. But if you get a little nibble now and again, you say that's not too bad and that's it.

When a young man's sexual advances were rejected his frustration in the heat of the moment was soon, it seems, tempered by a deep satisfaction that he had found a girl who was worthy of his love and marriage. John Neary:

> In your courting days it's always a battle and if the girl is crafty and uses her loaf she'll always avoid you accomplishing what you're after, sex or whatever. It's a battle all the time; you're always ambitious, but the next day you're glad that you never did. We had five years' courtship and there were many times when I said, 'I'm not going to have this no more, I'm going somewhere else.' But you didn't, you didn't. The man is the hunter, isn't he? And any man who isn't ambitious in that field as a young man, and I was about twenty, must have something wrong with him. But if the girl was the same way, I think it causes problems, because you wouldn't have prepared yourself and she'd be in trouble. We had lots of arguments over this. 'I've had enough of this, I'm going

home,' but I think I would have respected her less if she'd given way.

The virginity of the bride-to-be was widely seen as a sacred part of the courtship ritual and it remained a powerful force in the early 1950s when Geoffrey Gorer surveyed British attitudes to sex in *Exploring English Character* (1955). He discovered that 63 per cent of the population were against any sexual experience before marriage – especially for women. The five most popular reasons given for this view were in order:

1) marriage should be a new experience;
2) the man wants a virgin wife;
3) the man should be pure because he wants his wife to be;
4) it is against morality;
5) it is against religion.

Further evidence of the sacred view of virginity was provided in Slater and Woodside's sex survey which focused on couples who for the most part courted during the inter-war years. They discovered that of all the men they interviewed who claimed to have had sex before marriage something like 40 per cent did not have sex with their wife-to-be. If this evidence is anything to go by it suggests that a significant number of men who were sexually experienced greatly prized the virginity of their sweethearts. They had sexual affairs before courting seriously, but chose to settle down with one who had denied them sex till then and would remain a virgin until marriage.

While convention deemed that young couples be chaste until their wedding night, we know that many weren't. But when it comes to counting the heads of the 'fallen brides and grooms' we are moving into very murky territory. The British sex surveys suggest that by the mid-century roughly a half to two-thirds of married men, and a third to a half of married women were prepared to admit to having had sex before marriage. Among young women most of this sexual experience tended to be with future husbands. Slater and Woodside found that less than 4 per cent of the women they interviewed had pre-marital sex with men other than their husbands-to-be, and in the Mass Observation survey it was only 10 per cent. Eustace Chesser's survey also noted that most women who had sex before marriage did so with their future husbands. His survey also revealed that 18 per cent of women who had pre-marital sex did so between the ages of thirteen and seventeen; 44 per cent were eighteen to twenty; 32 per cent were twenty-one to twenty-five; and 6 per cent were twenty-six or over. Among men the surveys found a greater proportion of pre-marital sex with women other than their future wives.

The age at which young women were initiated into this furtive world of sex before marriage depended very much on their social class. Sexual experience was closely tied to serious courtship prior to marriage and the age of marriage was, in turn, largely shaped by class background. The unskilled and semi-skilled working classes earned their best wages in their late teens and early twenties and had relatively low expectations as to where and how they might live, so they tended to marry then. The professional middle classes, however, who, because of a lengthy education and training period often didn't start to earn good money until their late twenties, often postponed their marriages until then, when they could afford to live independently of parents in the style to which they were accustomed. Eustace Chesser's survey on women's sexual experiences provides strong evidence of this. The great majority – 81 per cent of the respondents in his survey – from a working-class background who had sex before marriage did so before the age of twenty-one. On the other hand, the survey revealed that more than half of the respondents from a middle-class background were still virgins at the age of twenty-one.

Given the fact that young women had so much to lose from sex before marriage the question of why some agreed to sex while others resisted is an interesting one to raise here. All kinds of motives seem to have come into play. Romantic love and desire, the wish to please a lover, and the search for an intimate relationship to escape from an unhappy home, were particularly common. Perhaps, more surprisingly, illicit sex sometimes seems to have been bound up with a rebellion against oppressive parental control. Where parents used Draconian measures to control their daughters – for example, beatings, locking them out or locking them in at night – a not unusual response of girls was to rebel. Often the sexual rebellion was confused and carried out in the aftermath of an upsetting battle with the parents. Janet Baker was born in 1899 and spent her young days in the village of Baddeley Green in Staffordshire:

> In those days sex was not known as such, or intercourse, it was called 'having connections'. I was very innocent of these goings on. My mother told me nothing but we were told if we brought any trouble home we were doomed to the workhouse. . . . My second chap tried to have connections the first time. I finished with him. I had several in between but all were the same so they were finished. . . . And now at twenty-three years I went out one Saturday night and my chap and I were late coming in, ten past ten. My father locked me out. I sat all night in the closet, the toilet, and my mother let me in at six o'clock in the morning. I was allowed one slice of dry bread and cold water. That broke my spirit and I was very upset. I went out and sat in the fields all day. I met my chap next night and told him all about it. He wanted sex, so foolishly, under stress, I gave in. Three weeks later I found I was pregnant. I was eight weeks gone when we were married.

Some women agreed to sex for fear of being 'left on the shelf' and suffering the stigma of being a 'spinster' or an 'old maid'. This was an especially important motive among older women who found most of their contemporaries had married before them. Betty Milton was born in Manchester in 1904, brought up in an orphanage, and entered domestic service just after the First World War:

> The lad who used to bring in the foodstuffs from the shop, the errand boy, eventually started asking me out. I didn't care for him, but I was then twenty-six, I began to consider myself left on the shelf, an 'old maid'. He started taking me out and neither of us had much in the way of money, so we started spending time at his mother's home when she was out. This of course led to the eventual sex. I hated it but at twenty-six I was dead scared of losing him. In the end we were caught by, of all people, his mother. She called me all the unspeakable names she could, not a word about it to her dear son. It was expected of men, but decent girls just didn't do such things. I never even thought about him getting me pregnant, so no precautions were taken. I guess I'd just been very, very lucky. I used to hide anywhere when he came to the house with the groceries. But eventually we got together again; park benches, anywhere, hidden away, our sexual activity took place. Eventually his mother told my employer that I was chasing after her dear son. This Jewish lady told me I was being silly and that I could end up being pregnant by him, what then? Only then did I realize, but he sweet talked me round, saying he'd marry me.

Some men seem to have regarded sex as their 'right' once they were engaged and had formally declared their intentions of marrying. The refusal of a young woman to agree to sex in these circumstances could bring an engagement to a dramatic end. Resistance in such a situation required considerable courage, for a broken engagement damaged a woman's future marriage prospects far more seriously than a man's. The woman was widely seen as 'damaged' or 'shop soiled' goods. Gina Baker, the daughter of a London publican born in 1895, worked as a clerk in the civil service and, after her first serious courtship, became engaged during the early stages of the First World War:

> Well, I went with Arthur Sterne for eighteen months. We were very very close. I liked him very much and I thought he was very much in love with me. He was an officer in the army stationed at Winchester and I went to Winchester for a holiday and while I was there he took me out and he wanted to have what I wouldn't give him. I was frightened, I was scared because I didn't know much about sex in those days. All I knew was that if you did anything wrong then you had a baby, and that I didn't want. After we came out of the theatre, it was a bit late and we had to pass a park, and he said, 'Come on, sit down here a minute' and he started. Then he said, 'Oh, come on,' and I said, 'No, no, no.' And we had a terrible

row and he slapped my face. But when this happened I gave him up; I'd said 'No', he tried two or three times and I said I wouldn't give in and we had two or three rows and thought it was best to end it. So I gave him back his rings and presents and that was that.

Some young women were forced into sex against their will. Male sexual aggression or violence was probably never far below the surface in many relationships. Writers of sex manuals constantly warned newly wed husbands not to give way to pent-up emotions by raping their wives on their wedding night. Some young men, however, could not wait until their wedding night and resorted to sexual violence in order to get their way. Several interviewees recall being raped by their boyfriends or fiancés. Rape has historically been one of the most under-reported of all crimes of violence because police procedures and the law have been heavily weighted in favour of the accused as opposed to the victim. And within this subterranean world of sexual crime, assaults by lovers probably form one of the most unreported and widespread crimes of all. For this type of assault was most open to the common accusation that the woman invited and willingly surrendered to sex. Many women kept quiet because they were trapped by a web of duty, guilt and fear. Manchester factory worker, Emily Downton, was raped in 1946 at the age of nineteen:

My sailor boyfriend, as he was at the time, took advantage of myself, in actual fact in the front parlour of the place where I lived with my mother and step-father. I was not willing and we had not gradually got to the stage where the act of love was carried out. He forced me against my wishes. I loved him then so I kept my secret. It was just the once and never again until we married. He was more keen than I was; in fact, I did not wish to give of myself until marriage. It was not an enjoyable experience. I felt very guilty, yet knew I had done all I could to stop it. I felt cheap, very cheap. No contraception was used. I was aware that a baby could follow. I did not want this, for out of wedlock it was such a sin in my young days. I did not think that a baby could follow so easily after one enforced act of sex by one partner in particular. In fact, I did not even know at nineteen years of age how a baby was born. My sailor boyfriend informed my step-father that I was pregnant, but at this stage it had not been confirmed; I was being sick and just wondered if I had suffered the loss of the monthly cycle due to shock as I did . . . when I lost my own dad at fifteen years of age. My step-father told my mother what he had learned. My mother went off the deep end. She said that a name was given to people like myself. She suggested I had the child adopted and also go to an unmarried mother's home to have the child. I stated I could not give my child up for adoption. She then told me that only by being respectably married could I keep the child and the child would be illegitimate out of wedlock and scorned all its life. I must add, she

Pioneer birth control caravan of the 1920s. Young unmarried couples found it difficult, or impossible, to obtain contraceptive advice at this time

was a really good mother but with her strong moral values, she was upset and angry. She knew my sailor boyfriend was far more worldly wise than I was. I was really a child and looked it.

Where sex did occur among courting couples there were enormous risks of producing an unintended baby. Because of the taboo on sex many couples were completely ignorant of the risks they were taking. Others found it difficult or impossible to obtain contraceptives or contraceptive advice from doctors, clinics and chemists. For birth-control for married couples, let alone the unmarried, was barely respectable during the inter-war years. Many doctors refused or did not know how to give contraceptive advice to patients. And by the early 1930s there were still only little more than a dozen family planning clinics scattered around the country, the legacy of Marie Stopes's campaign to provide safe contraception for women – principally through fitting the cap. These clinics, like the state-run maternity centres which increasingly offered contraceptive advice to mothers, had no dealings with the unmarried. Indeed it was only in the 1950s that the Family Planning Association began to give contraceptive advice to single women, and then it was restricted to those about to be married. Evidence of marriage intentions was often required and clinics in Lancashire demanded a 'certificate from the vicar'.

So contraception was often left largely to the young man. The most popular method among married men had long been the sheath or condom, which could be bought at most chemists or barbers. But since it was not the done thing for unmarried men to be having sex they had great difficulty in getting their hands on them. Some chemists, who were often well-known and respected members of the local community, took a stern moral line on sex before marriage by refusing to serve young men known to be single. Bill Sides, who was courting in an East Durham mining village in the 1930s, remembers: 'I called into the local chemist's shop and asked for a packet of Durex. The old chemist blew his top and threatened to tell my parents. I had forgotten he was a chapel preacher.'

The embarrassment of being refused or of parents being told added to the terror that many young men must have experienced buying contraceptives from the chemists. Some people remember losing their nerve at the last minute, especially if someone else came into the shop, and they would buy a tuppenny toothbrush instead and leave, disconsolate. One popular way of avoiding embarrassment was to write down the order and pass it to the assistant. But even this ploy might require some persistence as Jack Baker, a young footman working in a country house in Dorset in the 1920s, remembers:

> We were nervous, a young unmarried man having the cheek and nerve to go into a chemist's and ask for that. But, when one comes to think about it, it was a commodity that they had for sale and they wanted to sell it, didn't they? The first time I went to the chemist's I had the bright idea of writing it on a postcard. 'Please could you supply me half a dozen contraceptives that gentlemen use.' That was what I wrote down. Handed it over and the chemist promptly handed it back and said, 'We don't keep that sort of thing.' Whether that was true or not I don't know. So I found a chemist that did sell that sort of thing and got on very well. After the first time I just used to take in an empty packet. 'I'll have half a dozen of these please.'

Barbers seem to have had less interest in the morals of their young customers, and some bought contraceptives after a haircut. But most young people didn't use them at all. Living memory suggests that withdrawal was by far the most common form of birth-control used among courting couples. It was felt to be more intimate and natural than sex with contraceptives and it was a way of avoiding all the embarrassing rituals of the chemist's shop. But it was also, of course, much more unreliable and dangerous. Not all girls were aware how dangerous it was but most had a sense that it wasn't safe.

Although many young women were aware they were taking a risk having sex before marriage, few were probably aware of how great the risk of pregnancy was. To get a rough idea of what this risk was it is tempting to play around with some of the admittedly very crude

Choosing a wedding ring in
London during the Second World
War. This ritual became
increasingly important as the big
church wedding grew both in
importance and popularity
through the century

statistics that we have looked at in this chapter. If we combine the tentative pre-bridal pregnancy rate of 20 per cent, with the equally tentative findings of the major British sex surveys which suggest that almost 40 per cent of women had sex before marriage during the first half of our century, we come up with a remarkable statistic. At least one out of every two women who risked pre-marital sex got pregnant. If we add to this the 4 or 5 per cent of illegitimate births each year, the chances of getting pregnant before marriage become even greater.

Disastrous mistakes with contraception – or the lack of it – sometimes ended up shattering the dreams of courting couples. One dream, dear to the heart of many couples, was of a perfect wedding, above reproach. This meant, more than anything else, that the bride should be chaste and virginal, or, more important, that she should appear to be so to family and friends. The big church wedding gained enormously in popularity in the first half of our century. By the early 1950s this fashion, which had originated among the Victorian upper classes, permeated all classes of society with more than half of all working-class couples being wed in a grand manner. Even the more humble Register Office weddings favoured by the poor were becoming increasingly extravagant affairs with more guests invited and a family party to follow. The wedding, and especially the white wedding, had become an immensely important rite of passage into adulthood for young people. It was also a major public statement of a family's status and respectability. The most damaging thing that could happen which could bring shame on a family was for the bride to be pregnant, or at least for it to be known that she was pregnant. In the early nineteenth century there had been far less shame attached to being a pregnant bride. Indeed, in some rural areas it was probably celebrated because it proved the bride was fertile. The sexual puritanism of the Victorian years stamped out these kinds of traditional attitudes and the proportion of first pregnancies conceived before marriage fell correspondingly from around 40 per cent in the early nineteenth century to just under 20 per cent by the early twentieth century. Although we should leave a considerable margin for error in these figures, they do point to a quite interesting fact, which is that in Edwardian Britain, despite all the sexual taboos – or maybe because of them – something like one in five brides were pregnant when they went to the altar. This remained more or less constant until the 1950s, though in his report for the year 1938–9, the Registrar General stated that 'nearly 30 per cent of all mothers today conceived their first born out of wedlock'.

The disreputable shotgun wedding – contrary to what many people today might think – was quite a common occurrence in the first half of our century. When a pregnancy before marriage was detected it was usually the young woman who bore the brunt of the family's anger and shame. The young man would often earn a harsh rebuke, but the stigma attached to his wife-to-be would, at least within the family, be more lasting. The shame and the secrecy were probably greatest among the middle class and the respectable working classes. The outcome would often be a very rapidly arranged wedding, usually in a Register Office, but sometimes in church, and nobody outside the immediate family would be told the shameful truth, though many would probably suspect.

Among the poorest sections of society the pregnancy seems to have been dealt with in a far more public way. This ranged from remarkable tolerance and openness – and usually the most relaxed attitudes were towards the young men – to the public humiliation of the girl who was 'caught out'. When in 1931 Larry Johnson, a nineteen-year-old Glasgow gang leader in the Gorbals, discovered that his girlfriend was pregnant and that he would have to marry her, he was not unduly concerned about telling his father:

> I was nae frightened because there was no shame about getting a girl into trouble where we lived. I remember telling my father (he had nae met her by then – in fact, my parents didn't meet her until the wedding day) and he just shrugged his shoulders, just left it up to me, sort of thing; it was my life. And there was no big secret about it, and afterwards the wife got on very well with my family, they became quite close.

If there was any disgust and disgrace it would again tend to be directed against the young woman, and a pregnant bride living in a poor area might find herself subject to some sort of public humiliation and punishment. At a weaver's wedding in Preston before the First World War, the pregnant bride was, according to popular memory, stoned on her way to church. The public humiliation was sometimes instigated by the aggrieved parents. The experience of Bess Owens, the daughter of a costermonger, born in Clerkenwell, London, in 1908, who became pregnant at the age of sixteen, vividly illustrates this. When her pregnancy was detected her mother was outraged – even though she herself had been a pregnant bride – and she dragged her daughter through the streets telling friends the shocking news:

> I was courting a young man and I was sixteen and he was twenty-one. And my mother looked at me and she said, 'You're getting stout,' because I wasn't a stout girl, so she said, 'I'll take you to the doctor's.' I said 'Oh, all right.' So we went up to the doctor and he pulled my eyelids down and he said 'You're anaemic. Have you a young man?' So I said 'Yes.' But I didn't know it was going to make a baby, that's how ignorant I was, 'cause my mother never told me anything. So he said, 'Well, I think you must be pregnant.' With that, my mother pulled me out of the doctor's, out into the Exmouth Market and everybody looked at us and she said, 'Would you believe it? I paid for her to go into tailoring and I've just found out she's pregnant and she's just turned sixteen!' So someone happened to turn round and

said, 'What about you, Emmie?' 'Oh, I was older,' she said. Well, I did get a good hiding and was dragged home.

In the weeks that followed Bess was barred from seeing her boy-friend and went to stay with her aunt who lived a few streets away while the family tried, unsuccessfully, to fix an abortion. Several weeks later a marriage was arranged and the costermongers with whom Bess had worked gave such wholehearted support for the wedding that even her mother – who was initially reluctant to go – ended up attending.

> She [mother] had a stall down Paddington Road and all the costermongers said, 'Oh, we're coming, Bess is getting married.' They bought me lovely presents, you know. And she couldn't help but come. So really we had the church packed, they couldn't hold another person; it was lovely. And you know what costermongers are! Being on the Monday all the flower girls were there, it was lovely, didn't cost a penny. The neighbours all gave me armchairs and things, and in the end I had a nice little home.

As the day when Bess's baby was due drew closer, there was no attempt to keep it a secret and she regularly talked about it to her friends in the street. And after she was married, living a few doors away from her parents, her father would give her some of the meat on his dinner plate so that the unborn child might be stronger:

> As I went along some used to say, 'Hello, Bess, how long is it?' And when I had to go down the hospital I always had a couple of friends and·they all seemed to take it in good heart. But just my mother, it hurt her pride. . . . The females were very kind to me really, and me dad, I suppose he loved me. And I suppose that's where a little bit of jealousy came in, because my father never ate his dinner when he found I was pregnant. He used to whistle out of the window, because we lived in the same street, then I'd go up. He'd say, 'There you are, Bess, I've a little bit of steak for you.' My mother'd say, 'I bought that for you.' He'd say, 'Well, she needs it more than me.'

What kinds of marriages resulted from the courtships described in this chapter? They were by no means as unsuccessful as one might expect. Bess Owens and her husband managed to bring up a happy and healthy family of ten children – despite starting off and staying on the breadline. Few of the marriages of those I interviewed or corresponded with ended in divorce – which reflects the very low rate of divorce in Britain before the 1950s. This statistical success should not be taken too seriously though, as divorce was – for a variety of social, legal and financial reasons – difficult or impossible for most couples to obtain at this time. Comparisons with the present day in terms of happiness of marriages are thus impossible. Because divorce was unthinkable, several interviewees, for example, remained in unhappy marriages.

An Edwardian working-class wedding; clearly every effort has been made to put on a good show. During this century, the fashion for highly ritualized white weddings permeated all classes of society

Sometimes they had married hastily to avoid the social disgrace of bearing a bastard child. Sometimes one of the reasons for the failure of these marriages seems to have been sexual incompatibility. The taboos on sex meant that they entered marriage knowing little or nothing about their partner's sexual needs and wants. In most cases, though, the couple's sexual expectations of marriage seem to have been pitched realistically low, so sexual fulfilment was not an issue that could make or break a marriage. This was especially true of women, some of whom continued to see sex as an unpleasant duty, probably much as their mothers had before them. A good husband was one who worked hard, looked after the family and didn't demand his conjugal rights too often. The attitudes that husbands and wives had learned in their childhood and youth carried on into adulthood. And the secret rituals of youth passed silently from courtship into married life.

After the theatre, in the 1920s

5

UPSTAIRS, DOWNSTAIRS

As a single man in the 1920s Lord Jessel was one of the many rich young punters who regularly frequented the fashionable 43 Club in London's West End.

> The 43 had very high-class tarts and people would go on from a dance and pick up a girl from the 43 for that purpose [to have sex]. Everybody knew about it, it was famous. You came in and there was a door, inside the door was something like the Box Office at the theatre and either Mrs Merrick or her assistant was there and you paid a pound to get in. And Mrs Merrick was a terrific snob and I being an heir to a peerage usually didn't pay. And if you took a girl away she cost a fiver, a lot then, as a matter of fact, in the twenties. You paid the girl at her flat where she'd taken you and I believe she had to pay Mrs Merrick a pound to be allowed to go there. There was dancing, it was a very good band, and you would ask a girl to dance and if you fancied her you'd suggest taking her home and she might, yes.

While young aristocrats had no problem in finding sex for sale in exclusive London night-clubs some of their young staff – despite a lack of money – were also not to be denied their sexual pleasures. There seems to have been no shortage of opportunities for sex below stairs for some young male servants in upper-class homes. Jack Baker was a young footman in a Dorset country house in the early 1920s:

> The first girl that I got interested in sexually was a young nursemaid, a charming little blonde girl and I did get very fond of her. And we did have a sexual relationship which fortunately carried on successfully, and no harm came of it as I know of. . . . It was such a big place there were always plenty of nooks and crannies you could get into. We'd do it in the brushing room down in the bowels of the house when it was quiet in the evening. And when the people were away and we were almost there on our own we used to enjoy ourselves in rooms that weren't being used – workrooms like the brushing room where we used to brush and water the clothes, oh yes.

Out of this upstairs, downstairs world of young aristocrats and servants there emerged sexual codes of conduct and a sexual tradition that was, in some ways, quite different to that which prevailed among most young people in respectable society. Great wealth, late marriage

Undergraduates and their rich
young friends enjoy a picnic in the
late 1920s. (Lady Marguerite
Tangye is fifth from right.) The
coming of the motor car enabled
upper-class students to escape
from the prying eyes of proctors

and the social isolation of servants all combined to create an atmosphere which encouraged a particular kind of sexual experience. What
was unusual about this sex was that it would often not be with a future
marriage partner but a fairly casual encounter, perhaps with a prostitute, a footman or a governess. This chapter tells the story of the final
flowering of this unique sexual world of the rich and its gradual
disappearance from the 1930s onwards.

Upper-class attitudes to sexuality stemmed in part from the distinctive upbringing that the children and young people of this class
generally experienced. It was characterized by an extraordinary distance and separation from parents, which could be both physical and
emotional. Children rarely saw their mothers. They were too concerned with their social duties and commitments to bother with them
for more than perhaps an hour a day. They saw their fathers even less
and they often became remote, authoritarian figures who some sons
and daughters met only by appointment. They were brought up in the
self-contained world of the nursery with a nanny acting as a substitute
mother. At the tender age of seven or eight many were packed off to a
preparatory (private) school. Then many would continue their education at public school usually followed by university, which involved
spending most of their time away from home. The schools of the time
rewarded obedience to authority and conformity, and many crushed
individuality. The public school ethos was all about team spirit and
loyalty to king and country. In addition, the education system was
rigidly sex segregated right through from prep. school to university,
giving girls and boys little or no opportunity to get to know each
other.

The effects of this kind of upbringing on the sexual indentity of the
upper-class young were many and varied. One was the encouragement
of homosexuality and lesbianism – as we will see in Chapter 8. Another
was the stimulation of an appetite for sado-masochism and hard
pornography for which the British were renowned. Then there was the
separation of the great triumverate of love, sex and marriage. But
perhaps most interesting was the tradition of young upper-class men
having their first sexual experiences with prostitutes. Typically their
sexual initiation would come while they were at university in their late
teens or early twenties. During the nineteenth century the university
towns of Oxford and Cambridge established reputations as centres of
prostitution. The soliciting of students by prostitutes was seen as a
major social problem by the university authorities and in early Victorian
times they recruited their own police forces to control students' sexual
activities. These were disbanded with the coming of a professional
police force but proctors – sometimes accompanied by ferocious dogs –
continued to patrol the streets, parks and taverns of Oxford and
Cambridge well into the twentieth century. Until the turn of the
century prostitutes caught with students were tried and sentenced by
vice-chancellors' courts. The universities even had their own cells

where these young women were imprisoned. Cambridge had a lock-up in the 'Spinning House' – the local workhouse – and at Oxford, prostitutes were detained in 'rooms' under the Clarendon building before being dispatched to the town gaol. The usual sentence was seven or fourteen days' imprisonment and punishments were rigidly enforced. In contrast the guilty students were treated very leniently – it was assumed that prostitutes were leading 'innocents' astray. Occasionally a student who was found guilty might be sent down, rusticated (suspended) for a term, or 'gated' – confined to college grounds in the evenings for a few weeks. But normally he would receive no more than a verbal warning.

Class prejudice and class segregation were so powerful in late Victorian times that it was automatically assumed that any town girl going out with a student was a prostitute. Controversies over the unfair imprisonment of 'innocent young women' for prostitution offences was in fact the key factor which led to the demise of these Oxbridge 'star chambers'. Living memory suggests that the suspicion and stigma of prostitution which was attached to town girls who went out with undergraduates, persisted for some time amongst proctors and local parents. Marie Hunt, born in 1891, the daughter of an odd job man, remembers secretly having to meet the Oxford undergraduates she and her friends were friendly with before the First World War:

> We used to meet them round the corner or at the end of a certain street or something like that, but nowhere near the colleges. And then we went for a walk, yes, we generally went up by Port Meadow way. Or in those days the canal was much nicer than it is now, it was quite a nice walk, and we'd go down by the riverside . . . my goodness, if my father ever knew we were going around with undergraduates we'd have been, well, we'd have been gated like they used to be, you see. Oh no, we wouldn't have been allowed out. . . . Somebody'd look down on you, you see, you were classed as not quite nice. And we did used to meet them but we always had to meet them round the corner and when they brought us home at night they had to leave us round the corner. They were not to be seen anywhere near our homes, well, it just wasn't done, you see. And if the bulldogs were about, you see, the men daren't be seen with the girls at all.

After the First World War prostitution ceased to be such a pressing problem in Oxford and Cambridge. A slight levelling in income and wealth meant that undergraduates were not quite so rich – comparatively speaking – as they had once been. Also a new breed of students drawn from more humble backgrounds was now entering the Oxbridge colleges. Women's colleges became established, opening up possibilities for friendship between male and female students. And the coming of the motor car gave students and their girlfriends the means to escape far away from the prying eyes of proctors. Prostitution continued to be important but now the undergraduate wanting to buy sexual experience would most likely do it on weekend or vacation trips to London where there was far more choice and less chance of getting caught. When Lord Jessel was a student at Christ Church, Oxford, in the early 1920s, he picked up a prostitute at Brett's Club in London's West End:

> I remember my first introduction to having a woman was through a boy who was a friend of mine. He took me to a night-club in the holidays and we both picked up a couple of girls there, prostitutes, high-class prostitutes. I liked the feeling of the body but the actual act I needed a little practice at, I think. It wasn't as satisfactory as I thought, but I improved later. . . . She immediately guessed [I was a virgin]. It was a bit bungled. I did know vaguely what to do but I didn't do it very well. I don't mean to say I didn't come or anything like that, but one didn't get it quite in the right place.

The daughters of the upper classes were far less likely to have sex in their teenage years. From an early age it was drilled into most of them that making a good marriage was one of their main aims in life, and that any sexual activity before the big day could spoil their chances. Virginity, or at least a semblance of virginity, was a prized asset in this market. To ensure that it was not lost, their social movements were closely supervised by mothers, governesses, teachers and chaperones until they were in their late teens or early twenties. As a result, few strayed from the sexual straight and narrow. These restrictions were made more palatable by the promise of romance and marital bliss made by novels and advice books of the period. Some, like Lady Marguerite Tangye, spent part of their youth in a sentimental fantasy world:

> When I was fifteen, I swore that I would never kiss anyone until I married, which then influenced all my deb days a great deal because I spent my whole time pushing men away. My uncle had a tutor down from Cambridge and I fell for him. When he went and kissed me on the cheek and I was rather sort of inspired and romantic. I went down to the woods and swore by a tree that I would never kiss anyone until I married, not knowing what it meant actually, because I'd never kissed anyone, but I thought it was a good idea. So then when I was a deb at eighteen, thrown on to the London season without any preparation, straight from a farm, of course every man made a pass at me at every dance. I pushed them all away, or sat in cars with them and fiddled around and refused to do anything more, to kiss them.

The great marriage market for the rich was the London season. It lost some of its old exclusivity in late Victorian times when the landed aristocracy began to embrace the new wealth of families who dominated the world of high finance and industry. But until the 1950s it remained an immensely important ritual for the rich, ensuring that a few families kept a fairly tight grip on power and wealth. Young

Debutantes being taught the correct way to pick up a handkerchief at a deportment school in Kensington, London, in 1925. This was part of their preparation for the formal rituals of the London season

debutantes were presented at court, then spent year after year attending dances, balls and social events with the aim of finding a suitable marriage partner. Many former debutantes during the first half of the century remember this grand courtship ritual as producing a lot of tension, especially when the parents were zealous chaperones. Lady Diana Cooper remembered, 'You always had your mother's eyes on you to see if you were dancing with someone eligible or ineligible. And most of my friends were ineligible.' Joyce Grenfell remembered a similar set of restrictions:

> I was never allowed out alone. If my parents were not going to the dance I was escorted by the family maid, who was Swiss, not much older than me, who made a lot of my dresses. She would take me in a taxi to the dinner party and then the hostess would have to see me home unless my mother or father collected me.

Many of us imagine that this exclusive social set were quite sexually sophisticated. One of the stock images of the twenties, for example, is of fashionable flappers cocking a snook at convention at wild cocktail parties. In fact, the trendsetters of the time tended to be older married women in their late twenties or thirties. In the gossip columns in the new glossy magazines single women were very much overshadowed by sophisticated and daring hostesses like Lady Nancy Cunard. In a sense women had more sexual freedom after marriage than they did before – a blind eye might be turned to an affair or two as long as the appearance of a 'good' marriage was maintained. For many unmarried young women from the upper classes, the stakes were probably too high to indulge in sex before marriage, except perhaps in the later stages of a serious courtship.

Many young men seem to have respected this pressure not to court disaster by risking sex with debutantes. One of the main opportunities that aristocratic young men had to make love to girlfriends was on the house party circuit where young guests were invited to spend weekends at country estates. Lord Jessel remembers the bedroom manners on this circuit in the 1920s:

> In those days the upper classes did not on the whole penetrate their girlfriends – just heavy petting, as I think it's called today, because I think they were frightened of having children. I think the men didn't want the girl to have a baby and of course the girls were terrified of having babies. . . . They had big house parties and there were a lot of people going to the ladies' rooms. They did not sleep with them, but cuddled, and the man would have an ejaculation, that sort of thing.

Lady Marguerite Tangye remembers that at some house parties the young people would be given considerable freedom but this freedom was based on what seems to have been a deeply felt trust that there should be no sex.

> You were quite often asked to the country for weekends and quite often with a boyfriend or someone you knew. And you'd all go down in different cars. We'd swim and go to point-to-points and things like that and if you were a bit attracted to someone you'd end up lying on the sofa with them when everyone had gone to bed. It just seemed a pleasant thing to do. We were all single, we were all debs and young men, there weren't married people at all. There was the mother of the house, she was the chaperone but she'd go to bed. You could go to a boy's bedroom in the morning and sit on his bed and wake him up, it was quite free. I do remember staying up in Newmarket with one man friend of mine and his mother sent for him and he was lying on my bed. The mothers were there and sometimes they interfered but mostly they'd gone to bed. They really expected all this to be going on, that's what everyone was paying for, for you to carry on with someone who had the right name and plenty of money and a nice country house. It was a market, so they weren't going to stop

The upper-class wedding – a frequent front-page feature in fashionable journals and magazines. The stakes were so high in the marriage market that many rich daughters dared not risk sex before marriage

The Lady

A Journal for Gentlewomen

LADY NEWSPAPER, LONDON
STRAND C105

THURSDAY, 16 FEBRUARY, 1928

OFFICES { 39 & 40, BEDFORD STRAND, LONDON

LAST WEEK'S BIG WEDDING

The Marquis of Hamilton and Lady Kathleen Crichton's wedding was honoured by the presence of the King, and the Queen joined His Majesty at the reception.   The picture shows Lord and Lady Hamilton leaving St. Martin-in-the-Fields

it. . . . If you were very much in love you would think nothing of lying in bed with someone all night and talking to them and saying you loved them and everything, and you'd be quite safe because that was their upbringing too.

For sex, young aristocrats often had to look outside their class. Some might perhaps have a one-night stand or a brief affair with a young shop assistant or seamstress who they met in a pub or club. More often, however, as money was no object for these young men, they usually preferred to find a prostitute where sex was guaranteed with no strings attached. Many had been initiated into the world of prostitution and smart brothels as students and they renewed these links in their courting days. The centre of this trade was in London where many young aristocrats were based, at least for part of the year during the season. Some of them, it seems, would go to a brothel after an evening of heavy petting with a girlfriend to relieve their frustration. Lady Marguerite Tangye:

> When you came out in those days you met young men of the same sort of class whose upbringing taught them to protect the girls, they were all eighteen and innocent. And so you knew or you sensed that you would be all right with them and they never went too far, but you led them on and it must have been very hard for them sometimes. I remember sitting in a car fooling about with one man and he said, 'I must get out and run round the block,' cool himself off, I suppose. And some of them would go to the Bag of Nails, which was a sort of quite smart brothel-type place.

By the 1930s the sports car (usually driven daringly fast) was becoming increasingly important in upper-class courting rituals

More often the young man would go on to a night-club where he could pick up a prostitute after having attended a society ball or dance until late in the evening. Lord Jessel:

> The most common thing, I think, was to go on after a private dance of which during the season there were a great many and being an eligible young man I think I could have gone to a dance three or four times a week if I'd wanted to. . . . I'd arrive [at the club] at one o'clock. It could be a very short night. If there wasn't one I liked there I just didn't do it. But there were one or two girls there I did fancy and who became quite friendly with me. I mean when I got there I'd say, 'Is Cissy here?' and they'd say 'Yes.' In fact, one or two I'd visit in the daytime, tea time. They came from various parts of the country, various social strata. There was one, the one who gave me clap, who had been married to a colonel. She was very posh and she gave me clap. The girls were not teenagers – they'd go from about twenty to thirty-five. . . . And very often one was in white tie and tails and coming home in the morning at say half-past three which was quite funny for onlookers.

The young men in this set had a good chance of catching venereal disease from the prostitutes they slept with. However, they were less vulnerable to its potentially devastating ill-effects. They do not seem to have been tortured with guilt about having contracted the disease – as were most people at the time – and as a result they took speedy action when they realized they were infected. Equally important, they could buy superior private medical treatment to combat it, treatment which was simply unavailable to the majority of the population. Lord Jessel:

> The usual practice was to use French letters with prostitutes for fear of getting the clap. A lot of people did get clap then and it was much harder to treat. I had it myself once and it was quite a lengthy treatment. You discovered it because you had an emission from your cock and it began to be painful. I went to a doctor and the treatment was putting something like a catheter up and then you were sprayed with a liquid twice a day. It took about three weeks. I took it home and told my parents. They were very sensible. The treatment was uncomfortable but not painful. Rigging up the thing was an awful bore because you had to put it up high and there was a tube.

Prostitution was in decline, however, in the first half of the century. The rich remained loyal to the 'oldest profession' longer than most other classes, but they, too, were frequenting brothels less often in the 1930s than at the turn of the century. One important reason for this change according to most commentators at the time was that more young women from the upper classes were prepared to consent to sex during a serious courtship. One of them was Lady Marguerite Tangye who by the early 1930s was going around with a rather daring bohemian set.

I didn't have what's called a hymen. I asked my boyfriend's friend in Dover Street, I said 'Buster, how do I know if I've got a hymen or not?' and he said, 'Stick a poker up and see if there's one in there.' That's how they talked, my friends. And I was innocent but I apparently didn't have one because I'd ridden a lot, so it was not a big deal. I was staying in his friend's flat and he kept banging on the door and saying if I didn't sleep with him he'd throw himself in the Thames. And he got into a terrible state. I didn't know what he meant but I adored him and he had no money and all his friends were my friends. And he protected me, he had all the birth-control things ready. I didn't know what he was going to do, I just let him get on with it.

Lord Jessel (centre) on holiday in Italy in 1926

While the bright young things of the aristocratic world were increasingly gaining sexual experience before marriage, many young servants above and below stairs also appear to have had some kind of sex life. We can be fairly sure of this simply by looking at illegitimacy rates. From Victorian times until after the First World War they consistently show a disproportionately high number of young domestics amongst those who had babies outside marriage. In 1911, for example, almost half of all the illegitimate children born in Britain were born to women in service. We also know from the records of refuges, reformatories and rescue organizations like the London Foundling

Hospital, that many of these young women had been in service with the well-to-do who had several servants. Characteristically the young woman 'in trouble' would not be the maid of all work employed in lower-middle-class homes.

The high illegitimacy rate amongst domestics gives us an important clue as to what kind of sexual relationship they were involved in. Servants lived in a very enclosed world. This was particularly true of those who worked in larger wealthy households. They would often arrive from a village community many miles away. Living in with few holidays meant that most of the friendships they had enjoyed at home would be broken. They were physically isolated from the outside world living on large estates or in exclusive town houses. Quite apart from the high walls which separated them from the rest of society they were subject to elaborate rules that restricted their activities and movements. One common one was that they should have 'no followers', meaning no regular boyfriend or girlfriend. Added to this they were frequently on the move with the whole entourage of the upper-class family: up to London for the season, back to the country in the winter, off on holidays to the Continent, and so on. All this made it difficult for them

Lady Marguerite Tangye dancing with her husband-to-be in a London night club

to meet and maintain a relationship with what they considered to be an eligible young man. The traditional places where courting couples met each other like the monkey run, the park and the dance hall were for the most part out of bounds for them. Because of this lack of choice and opportunity the men they were most likely to have a sexual relationship with would be those they met in chance encounters on the street or in a train, or members of the household itself. Since a servant might be dismissed if it was discovered she had a lover, the relationship would necessarily be furtive and clandestine. The parental supervision and public ritual of courtship which prevailed elsewhere were largely absent. All these factors made seduction and betrayal – sometimes producing an unwanted pregnancy – all the more likely. Betty Milton was a parlour maid in several wealthy households in the Manchester area during the early 1920s:

> I really found out about sex from the senior parlour maid whose bedroom I shared. My employer's son was creeping into her bed quite regularly. I was terrified of him. Eventually the girl became pregnant and was instantly dismissed without references, as a dirty girl. The young man then turned his advances upon me. I told his mother, my employer, who told me not to be such a stupid silly girl, but this son was quickly married off to one of his own class. I moved again to another family and by this time at twenty-one I had a boyfriend. I thought he was marvellous and I was very much in love with him, but I was still a virgin. I'd been taught at the orphanage that good girls don't let men touch them. That was the only warning I'd received. Eventually he found another girl and I was heart-broken. I moped about doing my work crying most of the time. The lady of the house, my employer, was away and eventually one of her sons soon took advantage of my inexperience and loneliness. He got me very drunk on rhubarb wine and I woke next morning in his bed. He told me he loved me and that we'd elope and marry. I believed him. My virginity was gone. Eventually, one of the other maids told the mistress on her return and I was dismissed instantly.

The classic image of the 'fallen servant' which often featured in moral tracts, charity appeals and novels was that of the country girl who was seduced by a predatory upper-class man – her master, one of the sons in the household or a casual gentleman acquaintance. This seduction of the innocent parlour maid by a social superior became a kind of folk myth from Victorian times onwards and its prevalence was probably exaggerated in the popular mind. Nevertheless, cases like this were frequently documented in one- or two-line entries in the records of the charity institutions where some of these 'unmarried mothers' ended up. In Edwardian times there was a new moral panic about the white slave trade, a conspiracy amongst merchants and brothel owners on an international scale in which innocent young women in big cities

A comic postcard of 1925 plays on the popular theme of 'hanky-panky' in the big house

WHERE IS THE PAGE, MARY?
HE'S HELPING ME TO CLEAN UP
AFTER THE SWEEP, M'M!

Part of a turn-of-the-century slide show, in which the master of the house is caught by his wife philandering with one of the maids

were duped into a life of prostitution in foreign lands. This traffic had some basis in fact but its scale was greatly exaggerated. It added another dimension to the sexual fear and isolation experienced by many young domestics especially those who arrived from the country to work in wealthy households. In 1908 Jane Thompson, then aged thirteen, left her home village of Severford in Oxfordshire to enter service in London:

It was rather a difficult time in those days. The white slave traffic was very in evidence and I think at that time I had heard about it but didn't understand very well what it meant. But I remember they were always afraid for me, you know, that I shouldn't go out. I suppose I was quite a fresh-looking country girl and might have been attractive and there was an occasion when I quite believe I

ONE PENNY.

STARTLING TRUTHS on the WHITE SLAVE TRAFFIC

"Sold for Gold!"

SUCCESS PUBLISHING CO., Plough Court, Fetter Lane, London.
5th EDITION.

Church Army pamphlet warning against the White Slave Trade. In Edwardian times there was a moral panic about the sale and transportation of innocent young women to foreign lands where lives of prostitution awaited them

could have been taken. I used to have to clean the front brasses quite a lot, and there were a long flight of steps going up to the house in Phillimore Gardens. A man used to come down every morning, and of course to me he was rather like the Kaiser. He had the sort of moustache that Kaiser Bill had and I think he was a German too. He wore a silk hat, a frock coat and striped trousers and carried a briefcase, and every morning he would go down at a certain time. I don't know if he went to his business or whatnot. There was the long flight of steps and then there was a little paving going along and then there was the gate on to the pavement. And I had to clean the knob of the gate. And I was there and this fine gentleman that was supposed to be, I had seen him a lot of times and I suppose he had noticed me, he came down as he got to the gate. I suppose thinking back on it that he said to me, 'Would you come out with me one evening? . . . I would give you a good time.' And I was flattered beyond words and I hadn't got to the point of saying yes or no when out came a furious cook. You see it was a half basement and she had seen this man from the window. She flew out and of course he went off. And she said, 'What did that man say to you?' And I was all sort of blushing and thrilled. 'Oh', she said, 'never speak to a man, never speak to a man.' I said, 'Well this is what he said to me.' I hadn't had time to do anything else. But I just wonder what would have happened. And of course I've been horrified since I grew older and heard about the terrible things that happened.

Occasionally, it seems, the master of the house would use his power and authority to rape a servant girl he had a fancy for. These rapes were probably rarely if ever recorded and the victim was seldom believed. One such case was that of Violet Dann. In 1929, at the age of sixteen, she left the children's home where she had spent most of her childhood to enter service with a wealthy family in Whitley Bay, Northumberland:

> Every morning I had to be up at six o'clock to put the fires on; in those days there wasn't central heating. This was so the master could have his bath at eight o'clock. I'd been there about three or four months and I'd go and fill his bath up. I was in there one day and I was bending over to test the water and he came in and he shut the bathroom door. And he slid the bolt on it. Well, in my innocence I didn't know what was going on and he pushed me up against the window frame and he started mauling me and that. So I said, 'Is the water suitable, sir?' and he says 'That's quite all right, leave it as it is.' And he was mauling me all over like and then all of a sudden he picked my frock up and did what he wanted to do. Well, he took my pants down and had sexual intercourse. I knew it was something that shouldn't be done, but I didn't understand about things; nothing was ever explained – what happened about sexual intercourse, babies or anything. I just

knew he'd done something he shouldn't have done. So I in my innocence, I knew that something had gone on but I didn't know what it was all about and I came out crying. I says, 'I'll have to go now, sir, please open the door, sir,' and as I came out he says 'Now don't say anything about what's happened.' He says 'Anyhow, if you do they won't believe you,' because of his position, you see. And I go downstairs and Bob Short the chauffeur he says, 'What's the matter, love, has he been telling you off?' I says, 'Oh no, I've got a terrible headache.' And it got into my mind what am I going to do, what am I going to say. I were confused.

A female servant was actually most likely to have a sexual relationship with a man from a similar class background to her own, often a member of the same household. The documentary evidence of institutions like the London Foundling Hospital points strongly towards this. What encouraged these relationships more than anything else was the late age of marriage of many domestics, both men and women. Many married in their late twenties or early thirties, partly because they were so isolated they met few potential partners and partly because they were so poorly paid they had to save hard for many years before they could afford to run a home of their own. The presence of so many unmarried men and women in their twenties under the same roof must have provided a great incentive for sex before marriage. Because the ratio of male to female staff was often in the region of 1:5, the young men had more than their fair share of opportunities for sex. The upper-class household was one of the few social settings where it was not uncommon for a young man to have a regular sexual relationship with a woman older than himself. Jack Baker:

There was housemaids there and there was one I remember, she was older than me, quite a bit older, we used to get together and have a mild flirtation and a small bit of lovemaking. She got very fond of me and I got fond of her. But no one expected it to be of a lasting nature, it was just a bit of fun between us. Marriage never entered their head, I am sure, never once was mentioned. For one thing we knew that neither of us had anything much more than we stood up in and it was the impression then that you had to have a certain amount of money to set up home, as it was called, which resulted in the young people of those days not getting married until they were nearing their thirties quite often. They couldn't afford to get married.

When it came to having sexual relationships with the female staff the young chauffeur was in an especially privileged and advantageous position. Normally he would have been issued with a smart suit or livery, but most important he had access to one of the most prized status symbols of the period – a luxurious motor car. There would often be long periods in a chauffeur's working week when he was not required by his master or mistress, often when he was waiting to pick them up. During these spells some, it seems, got full value out of their employer's car, using it to bait young women and to make love in, having driven to some secluded spot. Bill Phillips was a chauffeur in London during the late 1920s:

When you was a chauffeur you used to go round and drive along and I've had girls actually pay for the petrol to have sex in the back. I had one girl and we went out to Beckenham in Kent and I said, 'I'm a bit low on petrol.' And she said, 'All right, I'll buy the petrol.' All they wanted was to ride in the car in the back like a lady and you was their chauffeur. Then you pulled up in a field somewhere and you got into the back. I did have one, we was having sex and she thought I had a letter on until she realized I never, and she went mad. She put her hand down and found I never had no letter on. She said, 'You've come, you've come.' I said, 'I ain't.' And that finished it, she had to masturbate me in the end to finish me off. I never saw her after that, she wasn't the type I wanted. She was too frightened, she was frightened of being pregnant I suppose. . . . I'd be going along and just look at them, and they'd look at me, I'd pull up. They'd come up and speak to you and you'd say 'Coming for a ride?' And if they said no it was no, if they said yes, it was a ride for a ride. I never used to wear a chauffeur's hat so they weren't sure if it was my car or not. I only wore me hat when the guvnor was in there.

The servants who seem to have been most vulnerable to pregnancy outside marriage were, surprisingly, not the parlour girls of popular myth but the slightly older women who worked upstairs as governesses, housekeepers, ladies' maids and nannies. They genuinely considered themselves to be a cut above the average servant, priding themselves on their superior education and respectability, and they would normally have worked fairly exclusively in the houses of the rich. They were most vulnerable because they tended to postpone marriage later than any other class of servant. They sometimes preferred the shame of bearing an illegitimate child rather than marrying a man who was perhaps younger and socially inferior to themselves – as many male servants would have been. And some were victims of the regular movement of male staff from one house to another in search of better pay and conditions.

By the 1930s the distinctive sexual world of the upper crust and their servants was past its prime and was being drawn rapidly into line with conventional standards. Many new developments were weakening the old sexual traditions of the upstairs, downstairs way of life. Fewer servants were needed. In the horse-drawn era the grand life style of every wealthy family was sustained by an army of low-paid servants. But in the modern age when cars replaced carriages and labour-saving devices took over many of the menial tasks once performed by hand,

A chivalrous young lover carries his lady ashore after a punting trip down the Thames, near Richmond, in 1925

droves of grooms and maids became surplus to requirements. Also higher taxation and higher wages meant that some well-to-do families could no longer afford to employ a large staff. The number of private servants in Britain dipped from one-and-a-half million in 1911 to just over a million in 1931, to under half-a-million in 1951. As domestics disappeared so did many of the old sexual practices that had emerged from their social world. After the Second World War servants no longer loomed large in illegitimacy statistics as they had for so long. Similarly in a more democratic age upper-class young men had to be more careful about their public image. If they wished to associate with prostitutes and frequent brothels they would do it more discreetly than in the past. But as the season declined and as the old semi-arranged marriages became less and less important, there were more opportunities to enjoy sexual relationships with young women of their own class. By the time of the 'swinging sixties' the old era of male sexual power and privilege based on rigid class distinction and equally rigid ideas of the innocent and dutiful deb was fast becoming a memory.

STREET GANG SEX

In 1929, at the age of seventeen, Larry Johnson was one of the Beehive, a notorious street gang about sixty strong in the Gorbals area of Glasgow. He had just completed his first prison sentence – sixty days hard labour for breaking and entering – which won him enormous kudos amongst the gang. The son of a warehouseman and a conscientious objector, he worked as an apprentice boilermaker. But his real life was on the streets. Most evenings he would be out until midnight on his patch of the Gorbals talking, singing, dancing, gambling, fighting and sometimes thieving with the Beehive boys. Attached to the gang were a dozen or so girls and Larry prided himself on his sexual prowess with them:

> In those days there was always a greater danger of getting girls pregnant, but there were always girls that did nae care. Busby Kate was the first one I went with. She more or less looked for noted members of the gang, she'd do anything for you in the way of sex. We had sex, very often, in what they called the close of a tenement – the close is the entrance to it. You'd put the gaslamp out and it was nice and dark, then you'd get in an embrace up against the wall and do it. It was all over in a flash. I don't think the girls got as much satisfaction out of it as the boys, because just as they were starting to get going, we'd be finishing. Nobody bothered you. The people who lived there just walked past you. I suppose they'd done the same in their young days. And the police did nae take any interest in it. They were quite happy to see us out of the way in the close rather than outside on the street causing trouble and breaking into places.

The older street gang, with its band of loyal followers aged between their mid-teens and early twenties, was probably one of the most sexually 'promiscuous' groups of young people in British society from late Victorian times onwards. Most towns and cities, and even some villages, had gangs like the Beehives. Characteristically they sprang up in urban ghettos and poor working-class communities, where most young people drifted in and out of them in their teenage years. In some cities, particular gangs caught the imagination of young people and they mushroomed into local youth cults with a style of dress and a style of rebellion that remained in fashion for anything up to fifteen years. This chapter tries to throw some light on the sexuality of these defiant young people.

Manchester was the home of the first modern youth cult, the Scuttlers, who emerged in the late 1870s. They were succeeded by the Ikey Boys in the early 1890s and the Napoo who became a cult in the Ancoats area in 1916. Birmingham produced the Peaky Blinders of the 1880s and 1890s and the Bowler Hats of the early 1930s. Glasgow spawned a host of local gangs and cults from Edwardian times onwards, amongst whom were the Redskins, the South Side Stickers, the Billy Boys and the Beehive. And from the streets of London emerged the Hooligans, originally a gang and then a cult south of the river in the 1890s. By the time Queen Victoria died in 1901, hooligan had become a generic term of abuse used regularly in the popular press to denote any street gang or rebellious activity in which young people were involved.

The sexual side of this rebellion on the streets has remained the most subterranean of all the traditions of young people. What little we know of this nether world of the slums has until now suggested that most of the action focused around minor crime and ritualized violence. Pilfering, petty theft, gambling, conflict with the police and territorial battles with rival gangs are the main events described in the few documentary and oral history descriptions we have of this street culture. All these activities, rooted as they were in poverty and inequality, were undoubtedly important in gang life, but so was another more secretive one – sexual relationships.

The accepted view of the sexual life of the teenage boys and girls who peopled the streets in the evenings is that it was practically nonexistent, partly because of a kind of sex segregation upheld by the young people themselves. Boys inhabited their own world, with their own interests, games and friends, and girls inhabited theirs, which was more home based. Any contact between the sexes, so the argument goes, was highly ritualized, usually taking place on monkey runs on weekend evenings when teenage boys and girls paraded up and down main streets dressed in their nattiest clothes trying to attract each other's attention. The friendships that were formed, it continues, rarely went beyond kissing and cuddling unless they flowered into a serious courtship. This picture, it must be said, is in many ways an accurate one, but it is a picture not of all gangs but of younger ones, of boys and girls aged fifteen or less. The life style of the older gangs who at weekends inhabited bars, dance halls and billiard saloons was rather different. The division and suspicion between the sexes continued, but there was a greater interest in having a 'girlfriend' or 'boyfriend' and a greater sophistication, which included, for many of those in or associated with these gangs, sexual experience.

This sexual experience is clearly revealed in the memories of those who were once attached to older, semi-delinquent gangs many years ago. It has remained hidden for so long, partly because few of the investigators and reformers who tried to document working-class life actually knew what was going on. Crime, vandalism and street fighting

A gang of unemployed youths, pictured in the mid-1930s. The older street gang was probably one of the most promiscuous groups of young people in British society

were in a sense public actions which were visible and to some extent measurable, but sexual relationships were much more private affairs, even if the sex act often took place in the street, in darkly lit alleyways. This was something, given the moral atmosphere of the time, that gangs were understandably very secretive about. Some investigators inadvertently assisted in this cover-up. Such was the moral prudery of the period that even when they detected 'promiscuous' sexual activity, they often could not bring themselves to actually describe it as such – possibly for fear of shocking readers or being censored. The youth worker Charles Russell's portrayal of Manchester boys published in 1905 provides a vivid example. He described the gangs of Scuttlers in days gone by as 'very bad', but believed that the basic instincts which underlay their battles on the streets were 'natural and healthy'. In contrast, he saw nothing good in the Scuttlers' successors, the Ike, who were less interested in street fighting and his condemnation of them centred around a veiled reference to their sexual indulgence: 'The Ike is a stupid fellow, who, from constant indulgence in vicious habits of many kinds, has lost control over his more brutal passions, and lets them have free play when the opportunity arises.'

There seems to have been two main kinds of sexual experience in the street gang world. First, there were very short affairs lasting no more than a few weeks, the swopping of partners within the gang and one-night stands, all of which involved only the most casual relationship between young men and women. This kind of encounter was, at least for the young men involved, seen in terms of sexual conquest and success – or pretended success – and was a symbol of masculine virility in the gang. John Binns was in a street gang in Finsbury, North London, in the early 1930s:

> Say you were a gang of about ten and you had say six girls, you more or less dared each other. And you floated off down the side turning and you did your stuff or tried to, then you'd come back. And you more or less threw your chest out, they all did, as much as to say 'I've had it away with so-and-so.' You probably never did, but that's what they used to do. And that's how most of the sex was done in my day unless you were serious and you started taking the girl to the pictures and spending money or even saving money to make sure you had a good weekend. . . . Those that had no experience or weren't bothered, they stayed in the same place all the time. They were classed as slow, that was the difference. But the bright boys used to float off for about ten minutes or so. Sometimes you took one of the other girls, you had one girl one night and then another. When you were in a gang like that you never had a special girl, you had one or two changes. If you heard footsteps you just made out you were fumbling about or talking, something like that. You made sure you never got caught and that's why I say it was a hole in the corner affair, you had to be very careful. I think it was enjoyable, forbidden fruit so to speak. Shouldn't have been doing it, so you enjoyed it, simple as that.

The other main form of sexual experience was in more serious relationships lasting several months or more. Here again, although a more affectionate and caring relationship was clearly involved, the 'girlfriend' often seems to have been viewed as a badge of male prowess and a reward for masculine power. Larry Johnson:

> The more deeds that were done by a gang member the more he was chased up by the girls, and there were a lot of girls like that. Now I was one of the hard boys in the Beehive gang, so Busby Kate wanted to go out with me. She singled me out, came up in

Despite various onlookers, a couple cuddle in a third-class railway carriage, 1900

the street and put her arms around my waist. And we did a lot of things together, dancing and going to the pictures. We went out for several months and from quite early on there was a sex side to it.

Sexual intercourse seems to have been a kind of rite of passage into manhood for male gang members. While most young people and society at large saw marriage as conferring a truly adult status upon an individual, male gang members viewed 'carnal knowledge' as transforming a boy into a man. To be able to boast of a sexual conquest, to talk intimately with the young men about methods of contraception and to worry about having got a girl pregnant, were what being a man was all about in the street gang world. The macho young men who enjoyed leading positions in gangs seem to have often possessed immense sexual power in their locality. They would relentlessly pursue young women from neighbouring streets who they wanted as girlfriends to the point where some girls who were initially uninterested gave way in the face of their constant advances. They would often choose regular girlfriends from the fringes of the gang or outside it altogether, partly because these girls were thought to be more sexually innocent and therefore supposedly more trustworthy. Bess Owens was born in Clerkenwell, North London, in 1908. For several weeks she refused to go out with the local gang leader who was later to become her husband:

> The funny thing about it, he was someone else's young man. I used to write love letters to him because he was in a school for disobeying [reformatory]. Because, during the war, he used to run up Exmouth Market and say 'Aeroplane!', and while they looked up, he took apples and oranges off the stall. So he got put away until he was sixteen. My girlfriend said, 'You write a letter, you know how to write a nice love letter.' But with me writing to him he came out and said 'I want to see the young woman who wrote this letter,' so she said 'There.' And I really hated him; I think I was a bit snobbish in my own way. 'He wears a cap.' And the boys used to bend their caps in them days and they always had their scarves round their neck and I thought, 'He's a bit too flash for me.' He used to play a mouth organ and all the boys used to walk behind him.

Lil Harvey, a teenager in Bristol during the 1920s, remembers how the reputation and popularity of a gang leader who pursued her eventually won over her affections:

> I hated him at first. He used to wait outside the Docklands Settlement after the dances and I used to go out the back way, sneak away, because he had a bit of a name with the girls I think, and I was afraid of him. Then one night I came home ever so nice, all on my own, and I got right to the top of the street where I lived and there he was under the lamppost. He'd asked my friend

where I lived and he left early and stood there to wait for me, and that's how it started. He just said he liked me and he kept asking to take me home and I wouldn't go so he found out where I lived. All the other girls did run after him and I was the one that didn't, and he was the one that was running after me. And I felt a bit jubilant that I was, you know, one over on them, so I started going out with him. He tried to get fresh with me the first time, the very first time. He tried squeezing my breast and he tried to go all the way with me. It was in the doorway of the factory at the top of the street and I ran away. I didn't bother to go to the club after that; I started going to another place, the Kingsley Hall, and he eventually found out where I was going and he used to be outside there waiting for me, he just kept pursuing me. So in the end I just went out with him, that was that. In the end I started to like him. I suppose it was the fact he wouldn't leave me alone. He was good looking and he was a good dancer. He was a laugh, he was a comic. He was so popular with both sexes; he was a leader, he always had a crowd around him all the time.

Once leading gang members began 'going out with a girl' they seem to have been much preoccupied with the idea that their girlfriend was their possession. Because young men often viewed their girlfriend primarily as a badge of status within the gang, they were very anxious not to lose face by being seen to have been 'ditched' or 'two-timed' by them. They went to much trouble to police and protect their girls from the attention of any rivals. After succumbing to the advances of their respective gang leaders, Lil Harvey and Bess Owens both found their freedom severely constrained. Lil Harvey remembers: 'On nights when we didn't have a date he used to sometimes look in to make sure that I was staying in, that I was staying in to wash my hair and not going out with anybody else.'

Bess Owens:

I think he was a bit demanding, he'd want to see me every night. I said 'Well,' when I thought I had someone else on the side, 'I think I'd like to wash my hair.' He said, 'Do that at a certain time when you don't see me.' He never took an excuse, he always made sure he saw me every day and he took me to work of a morning and he was there to bring me home at night. And perhaps when he arrived there at night there'd be another young man there waiting for me and he wouldn't care where he was, he'd hit him, bonk. 'Don't let me see you here again.' So I never had a chance with anybody else, you know.

As well as being seen as the individual property of whichever gang member they went out with, young women in poor working-class neighbourhoods were often seen as the collective property of the gang that controlled the 'patch' where they lived. A gang member who went

out with a girl from a neighbourhood controlled by a rival gang was, at least in tough inner city areas, taking a serious risk. His action was an open challenge to the rival gang's sexual power and was often strongly resisted. Larry Johnson remembers going out with a girl in the all-female Nudie gang in the Gorbals area of Glasgow in the early 1930s. The Nudies originated from the same neighbourhood as the South Side Stickers, who were the arch rivals of the Beehive gang that Larry led.

Turn-of-the-century courting scene in County Durham. Girlfriends were often seen as the property of gang members

> I went out with a Nudie once, Babsy Bain was her name. She was a well-known figure in the Nudie girls. She had a stall in the Barrows market selling whelks there and she was quite a charac-ter this girl. I enjoyed her company as well as the sex side of it. But I had to be very careful going out with her because she came from South Side Sticker territory and I was in the Beehive, we were their enemies you see. Very soon I learned not to meet her in her street because I got attacked several times. There was a wee bit of dusting up but nothing too bad because I was a great runner then. After that we did nae meet there anymore. We met in our territory where it was a bit safer.

The whiff of sex and violence on the streets of the ghettos from time to time prompted rigorous police attention, especially at moments of panic as, for example, during and immediately after the First World War. The police would maintain a presence – sometimes in plain clothes – on streets known as monkey runs where young people would congregate on weekend evenings. Invariably some youths would be moved on and a few arrested – often unfairly – for loitering, disturbing the peace or for minor assaults on girls. Fred Mulligan, the son of a labourer, was born in Salford near Manchester in 1901:

> I remember going down Eccles Old Road when they had the monkey run. We stood in the doorhole, there were four of us. I must have been about nineteen, and two detectives came up and got hold of us and said we were jumping on girls' backs. I was taken to Cross Lane Station and everything was taken off us and identification marks. Then we were pushed in the cell. They took our heights and everything, then we had to get bailed out. Eight people had to come and bail us out, parents plus the next-door-neighbours. And we got out at midnight. Then on the Monday morning at Salford police station court, we all got fined a pound a piece. In those days that was a lot. And we never had any respect for the police after that.

The picture drawn so far of the relationships formed between gang members and young women is one of male domination, sexism and ritualized violence. One puzzle is why young women from poor working-class areas became sexually involved with these men, given the way that they were likely to be treated. They would rarely be an active member of their boyfriend's gang. Girls formed only a small minority in the ranks of the street gangs themselves, and although they acted as weapon carriers or occasionally as decoys in raids, they were generally seen as 'too soft' and not to be trusted. Occasionally girls developed their own gangs, but characteristically the girlfriend would be drawn from the fringes of the male-dominated gang – often from the same street corner or dance hall that they frequented. One rather obvious question, then, is why these hooligans were not spurned *en masse* in favour of more respectable, law-abiding boys who went to church on Sundays and took the pledge with the Band of Hope. There were plenty of these about in working-class areas, though admittedly there were fewer in slum neighbourhoods. The respect for authority and conformity which these boys displayed were the values that girls were taught to admire at school, at church and in many families. Many girls from poor backgrounds did, of course, go out with boys like this and ended up marrying them. But interviews with both men and women strongly suggest that tough gang members were admired by many young women and they often enjoyed a high status in slum areas. Far from being repelled from these young men, it seems that many girls found them attractive.

By piecing together reports by moral rescue workers, the press and contemporary observers, and combining them with the living memory of those involved in gangs, we can begin to understand some of the attractions of the gangs for young women. The evidence of the Social Purity Movement is especially interesting because it did try to document the motives of 'immoral women' – immoral meaning not just a prostitute but anyone who had sex before marriage. Organizations like the National Vigilance Association and the women's patrols which were especially active during the First World War, mapped out 'moral danger zones' in many towns and cities. These were areas where young people were likely to be lured into sexual relationships. A small army of middle-class ladies engaged in street rescue work to save them and many girls were referred to rescue homes or 'preventive clubs' where strenuous efforts would be made to change their ways. The records of this rescue movement, when looked at critically, and when viewed alongside the memories of the people they were reaching out to, provides us with a glimpse into the twilight zone of the girl and the gang.

One of the main attractions which enticed girls to go out with gang members seems to have been the action and excitement which surrounded their life style. In an age when money was short and entertainments were few, there was very little for young working-class people to do – what excitement there was they created for themselves on the streets. The gang, with its defiant attitude to adult authority, was one of the main sources of this excitement. And the factory girls, tailoresses and shop assistants who toiled for long hours in monotonous jobs clearly wanted some kind of share in this action on the streets. Mrs

A quayside scene in the early 1900s. Organizations like the National Vigilance Association policed 'moral danger zones' like this, where young people might be lured into sexual relationships

Front cover of a popular magazine in 1937 illustrating the strong adult disapproval of the 'girl in the gang'

In horror, Babs heard her aunt giving evidence against her: "She's lazy and wicked—she runs about in the streets till all hours of the night with a pack of young fellows. It's time she was locked up!"

LUCKY STAR
THE NEW HOME STORY PAPER

2ᴰ

PREY OF LAWLESS MEN
An exciting New Story Begins Inside

F. Hay-Newton ran a Preventive Club for girls in moral danger in the capital just after the First World War. Her description of the girls she dealt with – which by the standards of the Social Purity and Hygiene Movement was extremely sympathetic – helps us to begin to form a picture of the kind of girl who was forming sexual relationships on the street. Like most other rescue workers, Mrs Hay-Newton believed that the girls who yielded to such temptation tended to be those who had been brought up in families where there was a lack of discipline and love:

No one who had not come to know these girls well would believe how few – even among those who have been leading an immoral life – are coarse, depraved or really deserve to be called bad. Some are vain and selfish, most are indolent; but they are, as a rule, well meaning, well mannered, and, to all appearance, respectable. That they are pleasant to look at goes without saying. Their faults are, generally, the faults of youth. They have warm hearts, high spirits, and – sometimes – sensuous natures. Is it fair to blame them because they have never been disciplined or taught the meaning of self-control and self-respect?. . . . To how many of the censorious has it ever occurred to consider the difficulties and temptations to which these girls, utterly ignorant of 'sex problems' and with little or no moral training, are exposed at an age when they are ripe for dangers that appear to them to have only the glamour and excitement of adventure?

Our picture of the girl and the gang comes into sharper focus when we listen to the memories of those actually involved. Doris Brown spent many Sunday evenings as a teenager in 'larking with the lads' on one of Manchester's monkey runs during the First World War when black-outs were often in force due to Zeppelin raids. Looking back she feels that 'the monkey run days were the happiest days of my life'.

Well, there was a little alleyway down Eccles New Road, chris-tened the Gully. There was always a gang of lads round this Gully, we used to call them the Gully Lads. Well then, there was another gang of lads that used to stand in what was the old Co-op doorway. . . . And there was always police, you know, plain clothes. We could spot them a mile off and we'd be off down the back, down Winford Street. We'd come back when they'd gone. They used to say you were loitering. There was an awful lot used to congregate and we knew everybody and everybody knew you. Well the other side [of the road] nobody used at all. It was only the one side which was called the monkey run. And it used to stretch from Cross Lane corner to Langworthy Road. No further than that. They'd turn back at Langworthy Road. All they did was parade up and down there until they seen somebody they knew, and when you saw somebody new, right, you got in a doorway until you saw the police coming then you were off. . . . Oh, it was fun! It really was fun. There was no lights and invariably we'd say, 'Oh there's so-and-so.' Well, it was nobody's business what we did, nobody's.

Minor crimes like 'joy riding' must have for many youths added to the sense of adventure and excitement of going out with the boys in the gang. Larry Johnson remembers:

I'd sometimes nick a car from town, pick up my girl in that, for a laugh you know. It might be quite a flashy one, we'd arrive in style.

'Dockland degenerate.' A popular 1930s image of the type of woman involved in criminal gangs

Then we'd leave it near where we were going. That was quite a regular thing but we never got caught.

Joe Maddison was in a street gang in South Shields, Tyneside, during and just after the First World War.

Talk about lads now being bad, I'll give you one instance. I'll be eighteen or nineteen at the time, and it was on a Bank Holiday Monday, and I says to the lads and lasses as used to go to Crown Dance Hall at South Shields every Saturday night, 'Come down to Mill Dam on Monday morning and I'll take you all to Wryton.' I went and stole a motor boat. Aye, it was moored in front of the police station and all, the river police station. And of course I knew who the owner of the boat was mind – Mickie Hanlan, the shipping butcher. I used to do a lot of work for him. But I never went and asked him if I could have a loan of the boat. I just went down and took the boat. I told the others 'Fetch two gallons of petrol with you.' And I took the boat, took them all the way to Wryton, to Wryton Willows for the day.

Another important attraction of the older gang member for the girl was the fact that he was likely to have money to spend on her. Unskilled and semi-skilled youths, who tended to be in the forefront of the gang world, enjoyed relatively high wages early in their working lives, in contrast to those who were starting apprenticeships or beginning office careers who tended to be comparatively low-paid. As young women were normally paid less than young men – of course both would hand over some of their earnings to their parents – they became to some extent financially dependent upon their boyfriends. The 'moral dangers' of this were highlighted by the Committee of Social Investigation and Reform in a survey called 'Rescue Work: An Inquiry and Criticism', published in 1919.

The moral danger of the girl is still further increased by the fact that she is usually dependent on a man for recreation, her earnings being too small to allow of a margin for amusement; and so she must be 'treated' to these or go without, and the nature of the amusements, late hours, but especially her dependent position, prepare the way for her fall; 'The four shillings a week of the girl of fourteen was soon given up for a life of sin,' appears in the annual report of one home. . . . But, unfortunately, it is not always possible to excuse the woman. Some girls are naturally light-minded and apparently without any sense of shame. They delight in admiration and in their craving for it and the luxuries that have for them the added attraction of the unknown, they are indifferent to consequences. Living entirely in the present and its amusements, such women drift easily into a life that has many allurements for them.

There were obviously strong incentives for a poor girl who wanted to dress smartly and enjoy a full night-life to go out with a leading gang member, especially one who dabbled in crime as did Larry Johnson:

I'd see Busby Kate a few times a week, we'd go to the pictures or dancing. I remember sometimes we'd go clabber dancing in the fields in Ballock – go there for a day out on the train. I'd usually pay. Our gang was very much involved in stealing from shops and warehouses so we'd both look quite smart. I'd have a suit, tailor-made out of cloth that was stolen, and I'd make sure she had a good supply of silk stockings.

Ray Rochford recalls that in the Salford slums of the late 1930s, young women also benefited from the booty of street gang crimes:

The gang leaders would knock the stuff off from the markets – watches, jewellery, brooches, handbags, frocks, all knocked off. And they'd give them to the girlfriend and she'd be parading about like a bird of paradise on a Sunday evening; three rings on, watch, pearls, white cork shoes, big handbag. And the other girls used to get envious, you see, because working for a living you

1930s club scene. For the girl, one of the attractions of the gang member was the money he would have to spend on her

couldn't buy anything like that on twenty-five bob a week. So it was all knocked off from the market or from the shops.

Gang members often pretended to girlfriends that they had earned the gifts and the 'good life' they were paying for through hard graft. For most girls wished to assume an air of semi-respectability and they would have rejected boys if they thought they were – or were likely to turn into – hardened criminals. Charles Rook, describing London street gangs in 1900, explained:

> It is a curious fact that the hooligan boy seldom finds an ally in his girl when he wants to be flagrantly dishonest. She does not ask too many questions, she does not, for instance, inquire where he got the money to pay for a hot supper after the entertainment; but she would prefer to think that her boy is 'in work' and 'earning good money', and she is perfectly capable of maintaining that proposition – with tooth and claw, if need be – against any other lady who presumes to doubt it.

The idea of being the 'property' of a young man in the gang – even if he helped you to get fashionable clothes – was, as we have seen, often viewed by girls as an unwanted imposition of power. But it did have some practical advantages. In tough working-class areas where violence was endemic, it could provide a young woman with a passport to safety and valuable protection from harassment or interference by other men. Ray Rochford:

> If a girl was known to be knocking about with say Tommy Dawson of the Dock gang, at the back of the Salford docks, well she was left alone, because she was Tommy Dawson's property, you see. Or Billy Gallagher, another hard case, if his girl went somewhere and a lad annoyed her, they'd say, 'Don't mess with her, she's Billy Gallagher's.' And he'd back off. That was the power. And it was a vicious brutal power, make no mistake about that. If Billy Gallagher got to know that somebody was messing around with her, he'd go round there and that guy'd be in hospital for five or six weeks. Because he was insulting him, wasn't he, through his girl.

In fact, some girls played on the young men's concern with sexual possession to wield some power of their own. It was often said that a girl would stir up the sexual envy of her boyfriend by accusing others or encouraging others to try to capture her. A fight for rights of possession or to protect her honour would sometimes result, and if the protagonist came from a different gang there might be a battle between the rival gangs. Such girls were known as 'bad girls' or 'troublemakers', and stories about their 'flirtations' frequently crop up in the folklore of gang life from late Victorian times onwards – especially stories recounted by men. The most vivid descriptions of the fights which resulted from their actions were penned by journalist Charles Rook in his book *The Hooligan Nights*, published in 1899. The book is supposedly based on Rook's conversations with and observations of a young south London 'hooligan', referred to as Alf, but clearly there is a semi-fictional element in his accounts:

> Young Alf was really in love this time; had been in love for some months, without a waver or a doubt. He had been walking with Alice. But when a boy is really in love, and is not merely mucking about, he is always a little ashamed of himself. That, I presume, was the reason why young Alf has said nothing of Alice for some time. But there was a rival in the case – one Ginger, who sold newspapers on the other side of the water. Alice, I gathered, had shown a decided preference for young Alf; but Ginger had been pestering Alice with unwelcome attentions and young Alf had sworn to mark him. Decidedly the evening promised fun. We passed from the glare and blare of the walk into a dimly lighted side street, under a railway arch, and halted before a narrow doorway cut in a big pair of gates. . . . A couple of lanterns gave light enough to show me a stable yard. A dozen or so of partisans formed a ring. This time there was no noise, no seconds, no towel flapping. Also there were no rules. They were fighting in savage silence. We, too, stood round tense and earnest, making no sound; for now at last we were breaking the law and disturbing the Queen's peace. It seemed to me a long time that I stood there watching the flicker of the lanterns on those two struggling figures. But probably only a minute or so passed before young Alf brought off his favourite manoeuvre in the kind of fighting where nothing is barred. With a quick butt of the head, and a raised elbow, he caught Ginger under the chin, and bore him to the ground, falling on top of him. Young Alf rose and passed his arm across his lips. Ginger remained where he was. That is an effective stroke if you have cobbles underneath on which to crack your adversary's skull. Someone brought a pail of water and threw it over Ginger, who presently sat up and looked about him. Outside, under the lamppost, I found Alice adjusting young Alf's neckerchief. 'You won't 'ear no more from Ginger, not for a bit,' said young Alf. 'Now then, come on; don't 'ang about.' They walked away together – Alice looked proud – and so happy!

There is no better material for the popular novelist than a fight between two young men for the hand of a woman and it seems likely that the reports of journalists and the memories of old people colour up and exaggerate the importance of this kind of episode, for the sake of a good story. Cecil Bishop, in his supposedly factual book *Women and Crime* (1931), took this fear and fascination with female sexual power into the realm of fantasy, when he claimed that women had used their sexuality to win control of many delinquent and criminal gangs:

157

If sex betrays a woman into criminal circles it is also her greatest weapon once the first step has been taken. Many efficient gangs, both in London and the provinces, are led by women, who exploit their sex to maintain control of the men they have gathered around them. To explain how these women-led gangs come into being a recent case may be quoted. A plague of thefts broke out in a London suburb. Despite a close watch, the thieves evaded capture and eventually became emboldened to attempt minor burglaries. At length it was found that the delinquents were a gang of lads under the leadership of a girl of sixteen. This girl had her headquarters in a disused shed, where she planned the coups, issuing instructions to her followers, who reported each evening at seven o'clock. Needless to say, she used her sex to gain ascendancy over the boys, but she did this in a peculiarly subtle fashion. Realizing that to make herself cheap would be the surest way of losing her influence, she chose the strongest and likeliest lad to be her 'friend', on the understanding that immediately he failed to keep the gang in order she would choose another boy to share the leadership. At the same time the rest of the gang understood that any member had a chance of supplanting the favourite, if he could prove himself a better man.

While exaggerated accounts of this abuse of female sexual power were largely fictitious, it does seem likely that some young women attached to gangs would from time to time orchestrate fights between the boys. It may have been that this was one of the most effective ploys they could use if they wanted to change their boyfriend or test his loyalty and commitment to them. The double standard was as much in evidence in street gangs as in any other walk of life and to provoke a fight must have provided sweet revenge on this predatory male dominated world. Ray Rochford:

The girls used to stir up the trouble in the dance halls. They'd say to their boy, 'That fellow over there keeps looking at me.' So they'd go over and sort him out. And they'd say, 'See what I can do, see what power I've got!' And that's what used to happen, they liked that you see. And then they could boast to the other girls, 'I've got the power over Big Tommy to make him do these things, I made him do that.' And the others would think, Wish I could get a lad in the gang who'd do that for me.

Finally, it is interesting to explore some of the sexual attractions of the older gang for young working-class women. Street gangs, and in particular youth cults, often developed a distinctive style of dress and hair which was both macho and erotic. Rebellion was partly expressed through style and fashion and their 'look' marked them out as something special in the drab, uniform and hand-me-down neighbourhoods where they lived. A lot of time, trouble and expense went into their appearance, and local girls were probably much impressed by their style. A letter received by the *Birmingham Weekly Post* in 1936 recalled in detail the remarkable Peaky Blinder style of fifty years before:

> Their clothes consisted of trousers twenty-two inches round the bottom and fifteen inches round the knee. Some preferred moleskins or 'cords'. They wore a silk 'daff' as they called it, twisted twice round their necks and tied at the ends. It was then called a 'choker'. And a bowler hat with the brim made to fit the sides; the front of the brim came to a point almost like the spout of a jug. This was done by wetting the brim, warming it by the fire, then making it a shape required. This was worn on the side of the head to show the hair on the other side done in a 'quiff'.

The dress of the late Victorian Manchester Scuttlers was vividly portrayed by youth worker Charles Russell. 'You knew him by his dress. A loose white scarf would adorn his throat; his hair was plastered down upon his forehead; he wore a peaked cap rather over one eye; his trousers were fusty, and cut – like a sailor's – with bell bottoms. This fashion of the trousers was the most distinctive feature of his attire and make-up.' The Scuttlers also wore belts with ornamental designs which were described by Alex Devine, police court missionary to lads in Salford. 'These designs include figures of serpents, a heart pierced with an arrow (this appears to be a favourite design), Prince of Wales' feathers, clogs, animals, stars, etc. and often either the name of the wearer of the belt or that of some woman.' The hooligan style in London at the turn of the century involved a donkey fringe haircut, a T-shirt, a long jacket, tight trousers and heavy steel-capped boots. The Redskins wore red head bands tied around their foreheads with feathers attached during their heyday in Glasgow during the First World War. This emphasis on style extended to the ordinary street corner gang which had no pretensions to 'cult' status. John Binns was in such a gang in North London in the early 1930s:

> We had special haircuts. You could have a long back and side but the favourite haircut that they used to have, they called it a 'DA', to be rude it's called a duck's arsehole. You had a little bit at the back of the hair that seemed to waggle and that's why they called it a 'DA'. And everybody went for that. And that's why you went to the barber's at least once every fortnight, that's if you could afford it, from sixteen onwards. The fashion in my day was what they called Oxford Bags, that was trousers that were possibly twenty inches across; they were really wide and everybody went for them. They were all in a grey flannel, or soft flannel, and they were quite cheap. And shoes, they'd call 'em winkle pickers. Fortunately I didn't wear them very often, but they're the ones that crippled you, they went right to a point. Sports' shirts were popular and one time, winter time when I was eighteen, the fashion was the bowler hat. And then the trilbies; they had various types of

trilbies, the flash boys used to wear them, and they looked like gangsters. I think the films had a lot to do with that.

Girls clearly found this stylish dress very attractive for they created their own street fashions helping to forge for themselves their own rebellious identity. In *The Classic Slum*, Robert Roberts recalls that Scuttlers' girlfriends had their own style of dress, wearing 'clogs and shawl and a skirt with vertical stripes'. The Napoo girls in Manchester in 1916 wore something very similar. As the cinema became more popular after the First World War girls began to draw more on Hollywood fashions when creating their image. Lil Harvey used to make a big impression when she went out on Saturday nights with her gang-leader boyfriend in Bristol during the late 1920s and early 1930s:

> I felt proud, like I was a gangster's moll. Used to go to dance halls with him. I used to dress very fashionably, and I used to make all my own clothes. My hair used to be jet black then. I used to have a fringe, and some of them used to call me Claudette Colbert; I was supposed to be very good looking in those days. And I took a lot of trouble especially over my hair. I think it was from the films where we got our ideas. I did put eighty-six curlers in my head every night, metal dinkie curlers. God it was painful to turn your head on the pillow. I'd put lotion on each strand, then put the curlers in – this was before the days of perms. And at the weekend I took hours and hours doing this so that I'd look the part.

It is difficult, if not impossible, to discover how and why the attraction of the girl for a boy in the gang developed into a sexual relationship – there is just so little evidence. But we can hazard one or two guesses. Generally speaking the accepted ritual of courtship allowed boys to make sexual advances and expected girls to rebuff them. What is intriguing is why many girls broke this rule when they went out with gang members. Living memory suggests that one important reason why they did was because there was usually more opportunity for safe sex when going out with an older gang member. Part of this came down to their influence on the streets. They knew the safe secluded spots to go to, and they could look to the gang for any protection that was needed from adult interference, for even the police would often not dare to intervene if they suspected illicit sex in the way they might with a more respectable younger man. Larry Johnson:

> We'd know all the quiet spots in the courts and tenements late at night. The police would leave us alone as long as we weren't out making a noise or breaking in somewhere. And once or twice if they did interfere we'd chase them. That was a wonderful sight to see the police running away.

The gang member would also create devious opportunities to be alone with his girlfriend – preferably in her home. Though frightened, many girls must have been seduced in this way, as was Lil Harvey:

It was in our front room, on the settee. I'd been going out with him for a few months. The funny part of it was every Thursday he used to have two free passes for the old theatre – they used to get them free for advertising in the shop. And he used to give them to my mother to take her friend, the neighbour next door to the old theatre. So Thursday night it was always safe. And then my little sister, he used to give her tuppence to go over to the Magnet cinema, so as we'd be there alone. He'd be round about half-past six, soon as they'd gone and they didn't get back till half-past nine. . . . Sex, I still thought it was horrible and I still thought it was filthy. It's most strange – I think it's why I couldn't have loved him. It was just him. I know I was scared, really scared the first time, and I thought he'd injured me. You know, that must have been when he – what do they call it? – broke the maidenhead.

Girls who developed an appetite for sex were likely to be more adventurous and would conspire with their boyfriends to create opportunities to make love. As a young teenager in the early 1920s Bess Owens had a remarkably liberal view of sexual relationships of the sort that would become fashionable half a century later:

My gran had lived with a man and she said to me, 'Never live with a man, Bess.' I said, 'Well, if I want to live with a man, I think they'd be the happiest time cos you're not married, you can walk out.' So she said, 'You've got funny ideas to me.' I said, 'Well, if I loved anybody I wouldn't care about living with them or anything.'

She went out with an ex-reformatory boy who had a room in a house further down the same street where she lived. At the age of sixteen, to avoid her father's ten o'clock curfew, she and her boyfriend devised an extraordinary plan to regularly enjoy an hour's lovemaking in the evenings.

Well, my young man had his own room. I used to say to his sisters, they lived in the house, 'I'm coming down to clean his room out or do the washing for him.' And they said, 'Oh, umm.' But they said they used to hear me go in at the wrong time to do the washing. I'd go there at ten o'clock at night when I should have been indoors. I'd been put to bed once. I slept with my gran 'cause she'd lost granddad, so she wanted me to sleep with her. She said 'If you don't read to me' – 'cause she couldn't read – '*Peg's Paper*, I won't let you go out again.' She'd let me get up and go out but providing I read to her. Mum was upstairs and I was downstairs. My young man used to go one, two, three on the window, I'd say, 'We're going now, Nan.' She'd say, 'Now you be careful or you'll get me into trouble.' I used to say, 'I'll be back in about half an hour, Nan.' Then I used to go into his house. He lived downstairs, so his sisters naturally heard my little high heels and they knew I'd been down there but we didn't care – I had to be careful 'cause me dad, he used to go and have a drink of a night – he liked his drink – and he always came out of the pub at eleven o'clock so I had the time between ten when he came and looked to see if I was in bed, and the time when he came home. And my husband-to-be said, 'Time to get out, Bess, have a little cuddle before you go to bed.' I said, 'I've been to bed.' It sounded funny. But I used to make it back and when my dad came in at eleven he said, 'Oh, someone said they saw you.' I said, 'No, it wasn't me, dad.'

The increased opportunities for sex in and around the street gang world doesn't seem to have been matched by an increased concern with or knowledge about birth-control. What little evidence there is suggests that many pregnancies resulted from their sexual activities. Some of the young men bought condoms in barber shops but withdrawal seems to have been the most common method of contraception used. Yet even though the girls involved were taking a great risk – often without knowing it because they were so lacking in sexual knowledge – there was still hope for them should they get into trouble. There seems to have been a well-established code of honour amongst the young men in all the street gangs that they were duty bound to marry a regular girlfriend who they got pregnant. This was probably because the young man would be a well-known figure in the neighbourhood, probably living at home and working nearby, and there were enormous pressures, partly from both sets of parents, to marry the girl. In this respect, a pregnant girl was likely to fare better than if she became pregnant with a young man living away from home, who was, for example, in the army or the navy, or who was a migrant worker, a lorry driver or a merchant seaman. With them the pressures to marry were far less and the opportunities for leaving the girl far greater. Lil Harvey, Bess Owens and Larry Johnson were all involved in 'shotgun weddings' in their teens or early twenties. There seems to have been an accepted code of conduct for street gang members in these circumstances. And if they broke the rules, violent resistance from the aggrieved party might result, as Larry Johnson remembers:

I'd been going out with the wife for about eighteen months when I got her pregnant and that was it. We got married. Because that was the thing on the streets in those days if you'd been with a girl for some time. There was no shame in it. It was very common in the Gorbals to marry a girl when she was pregnant; that was the main reason for marrying them. You dare not mess around when you got a girl pregnant. I remember, och, there was a terrible incident that made the boys very wary of what they did when they got a girl into trouble. There was a gang of girls called the Nudies and one of the Southside Boys got a Nudie pregnant and when she came to him for help he laughed at her and he said, 'Haun ne

A gang of lads with their whippets in a Yorkshire pit village in the 1930s. There were well-established codes of honour among gang members

naw', meaning go away. And she committed suicide, she jumped off a bridge into the Clyde. Now her sister took up with this boy for a night. He didn't know it was her sister but she wanted revenge. She let him get her up against the wall and he got it out and she slashed it with a razor. He did nae die but he was badly cut.

To grasp the meaning of illicit street gang sex fully it has to be set against the background of poverty, bad housing and social deprivation from where it emerged. Sexual experience provided these young people with a momentary escape and excitement, and in poor areas pleasures were generally taken as and when they presented themselves. It had the additional attraction of being free. Probably even more important in the minds of young Ikey boys and Redskins, was the power of sex to shock the respectable adult world. To taste the forbidden fruit went to the heart of their rebellious identity. Yet their rebellion did not call into question the aggressive and acquisitive attitudes towards women which were strongly present in working-class culture – indeed it reasserted them. These young men were just finding their feet as independent adults and to do this many adopted a defiant attitude towards their mothers who had brought them up. Many mothers cherished the sexual purity and respectability of their sons, and these were values which many sons set out to break – if only in secret. Sexual conquest became linked in many young minds with masculinity and with being a 'real man'. There were some similarities in the motives which drew young women into this world of illicit sex. They too were attracted by the gang's rebellious stance against society. And for some, sex was no doubt enjoyable despite the fear of being detected. However, it seems likely that for many more girls sex was a kind of trade-off which could – if they became a regular girlfriend – bring them status and security, entertainment and excitement, protection and even a little power. In a culture where physical force was important, where young women had few opportunities and outlets, and where the streets and places of entertainment were dominated by men, these must have been powerful incentives. Though taking a terrible risk of falling pregnant, the girl in the gang was actually looking after her interests in the way she best knew how.

7

BESIDE THE SEA

During the 1930s Walter Mack was a young clerk in Blackpool. He and his friends eagerly awaited the summer season when during their Wakes' weeks whole towns would close down and there would be a mass exodus to the coast:

> There used to be a Wakes' list that they brought out about May and I'd keep that and study it so that I knew where the Wakes' girls were coming from. Perhaps the last week in June we'd say, 'Oh good this is "Bacup week"', or 'This is Bolton week, they're not bad' or 'Hebden Bridge are here, they're all right.' That would be an ordinary conversation amongst working lads of a Saturday night. There was a lot of the mill girls that would stay in gangs of five or six in the large boarding houses in Albert Road and Adelaide Street, they were very independent those girls, they earned their own money and on holiday they pleased themselves. Of an evening they'd doll themselves up, I remember seeing them going arm in arm, making for the piers and the Winter Garden. When they got there us lads would be sorting them out trying to work out who we'd have a good chance with. Because at that time of the year you had a great chance of going all the way with some of these girls. Sex on the beach, it was a well-known thing in Blackpool, of course it was done in the dark. And I remember one of my friends wanted a bit more privacy so he used to rent a garage for two and sixpence a week and he'd put a settee in it. I don't think he thought it was a risky investment.

Inter-war Blackpool acquired a great mystique as a kind of seaside sex capital. For many young people it seemed like a haven of sexual liberty and licence. For the old it was widely condemned as a hotbed of vice and immorality. It was steeped in sexual legend: there was mass lovemaking on the beaches when the sun went down; there were secret doors linking single rooms in boarding houses; and in some hotels bells were supposedly rung early each morning to warn lovers to get back into their own rooms. Spicy stories like these were probably a popular topic of conversation in mills, factories and offices, and they were given added colour and credibility by sensational press reports of seaside frolics. Similar legends surrounded other popular resorts like Brighton, Bournemouth and Scarborough. And at the early Butlin's holiday camps it was widely believed – usually by people who had never been there – that night sentries roamed the grounds to keep amorous

Typical saucy seaside postcard. The seaside holiday came to acquire a mystique and become a byword for sexual licence

campers in their chalets. The seaside holiday – at least where young people free from adult control were concerned – was coming to be seen as a kind of ritual of misrule and midsummer madness. Far away from the trials and tribulations of the workaday world the young appeared to be enjoying a silly season in which Victorian sexual conventions were discarded, if only for one week in the year. Were most or all of these stories apocryphal, part of a popular folk lore of the imagination? Or was the world really being turned upside down on the beaches and in the boarding houses of Blackpool? In this chapter I will try to disentangle fact from fantasy in the extraordinary story of sex at the seaside.

The legend of the seaside holiday is part of an old tradition which reaches back a long way, and which possibly has its roots in the pagan fertility rites of spring. For centuries country people allowed themselves – or were allowed – at least one festival of pleasure during the spring or summer months. In the early nineteenth century most villages and towns staged some sort of carnival, sometimes lasting several days, where there would be much ritualized drinking, dancing, eating, fighting and sex. The most well known were the Wakes' weeks in the north and Whitsun feasts and revels in the south. There were also the hiring or mop fairs in many rural areas which combined employment for the year with entertainment. For many young domestics and farm servants this was their only holiday and the only chance they had to

The message on the back of this postcard, sent from Blackpool in 1908, reads: 'Dear Emma, My word, wish I was staying a month, you bet. Nellie.'

NORTH SHORE, BLACKPOOL.

I have had so much on my shoulders since I've been at Blackpool, that I get no chance to write letters, so postcards must do.

Exuberant bathers, 1905

meet boyfriends or girlfriends. Sexual relationships usually blossomed quickly, though there were probably not nearly so many as contemporary observers feared. In the early Victorian government investigations into the life and labour of the poor these carnivals were constantly linked with immorality and illegitimacy.

But the demands of the factory age and the rising tide of Victorian respectability and evangelicalism that accompanied it tamed many of these age-old observances. They became more restrained and respectable and by the late nineteenth century, allegations of sexual misconduct were quite rare. Traditional rituals of sexual misrule amongst the young seem to have continued longest in remote rural areas where pressures for conformity were often less intense. But those who remember these rituals remain very reluctant to answer questions about them. One of the few descriptions I have found was given by Shetland islander Robbie Fishman to a University of Essex interviewer. Robbie would only talk, though, when the tape recorder was turned off. The interviewer later summarized what he had said:

> He described to me then something which he called 'flatchie carding'. He said the girls, about six of them, would gather together after the sheep had been plucked in a barn of the house and they would sit there carding the wool (that's winding it round cards) until about midnight when flatchies (that is, straw pallets) were spread out on the ground so that they could spend the night. This was a signal for the boys to come in, and they would come bounding in and spend the night rolling around with the girls, jumping and rolling over them. I was only at one of those he added. He then said that later this custom was replaced by a fiddler being hired and people dancing into the small hours after a carding of wool. . . . When I asked him if the other members of the family knew, he said, yes, of course, they knew, and after all they had done the same themselves when they were young. I asked him were boys and girls more innocent then? No, he said, they were exactly the same as they are now. They were certainly not innocent.

During the Victorian age a new outlet for popular pleasures began to emerge – the holiday by the sea. This fashion began amongst the upper and middle classes earlier in the century. From their very beginning the pioneer watering places (as they were known) were surrounded with a suspicion of sexual misconduct. They aroused sporadic condemnations from moral reformers, partly due to the fact that nude bathing in the sea was then quite common. Fashionable resorts also acquired the reputation of being marriage markets or places where clandestine affairs might be carried on. Brighton housed a small army of high-class prostitutes and courtesans from Regency times onwards. But overall, the social tone of most watering places was demure and domestic – a home from home for the respectable middle-class family.

During the second half of the nineteenth century, however, the quiet gentility of resorts like Blackpool and Brighton was to be shattered by a working-class invasion. The extension of the national railway network and the introduction of cheap excursion fares meant that a holiday by the sea was now within the grasp of more and more families – if only for a day trip. They brought with them some of the carnival atmosphere of the old wakes and revels. At the same time, entrepreneurs great and small moved in to cater for the tastes of this new mass market, so that by the turn of the century the holiday-maker could enjoy a great array of entertainments and facilities which included fair grounds, fish and chip shops, piers, early amusement arcades and donkey rides. The new holiday by the sea was coming to be associated in many minds with a 'knees-up', 'letting yourself go' and 'letting your hair down'. Among the poorer classes this might involve boozing, singing, gambling, fighting and frequenting prostitutes. But most people had a more restrained and respectable view of seaside pleasures. This didn't include sexual licence. For above all, the seaside holiday was a festival of the family, a time when parents, children and sometimes grand-parents would all enjoy themselves together. During the Wakes' weeks in the Midlands and industrial north more or less the whole town – family, relatives, neighbours, friends and workmates – would all troop off to a favourite resort together. These family and community ties and restraints must have meant there were few opportunities for sexual misrule among young people.

It is clear from living memory, however, that by the turn of the century a minority of young people were going away for seaside holidays by themselves, often in small gangs or groups. Usually they were young men – often workmates – who would save hard to pay for a day excursion or a few days' board and lodging. It was less common for young women to go away mainly because of resistance from parents. In looking at holidays before the First World War I have had to rely on interviews in the Essex collection in which no explicit questions on sex were asked – so we can only guess whether the adventures described actually ended in lovemaking. It seems to me most likely that they didn't. To begin with many gangs of young holiday-makers had very little money. To get to the seaside, buy a few drinks and survive for a few days was an adventure and an achievement in itself. They would probably have been seen by most local girls as rough and undesirable. Frank Thomas, a former tinworker in Tongwynlais, South Wales, remembers how during the 1900s he and his friends would catch the paddle-steamer from Barry to Weston-super-mare:

> We were wicked devils mind. Every weekend we'd save our couple of coppers and then perhaps every two months we'd go across to Weston, from the Saturday till the Monday. And I remember when we goes over on the August Saturday we booked in a little place in George Street, one and threepence for bed and

breakfast. And we went out in the evenings having a drink and a bit of fun, and when Sunday night come we were broke. So we went to the landlady and asked her for our money back and she gave it to us, the night's lodge for that night. We slept in the toilet. And on the Monday morning instead of coming back, we started going around the sands singing in Welsh, collecting a copper here and a copper there, and we stayed there till the Wednesday. And on the Wednesday we lost our tickets, we had no tickets to come home or anything. We went to a pawnshop there and pawned our watches, and one of us pawned his waistcoat as well to have enough money to come back home. And in two months' time we had to go back to Weston to get our clothes out of there, oh yes we went back. But it was really good fun.

For those who could muster a bit more style and elegance than this, there was another barrier to sexual adventure – the seaside landlady. In popular mythology she was a fearsome figure, obsessed with the good manners and respectability of her guests. In reality she was often a rather more sympathetic character but nevertheless many did have strict rules about coming in at a 'reasonable hour' (usually half-past ten or eleven o'clock) and about keeping single boys and girls well apart – if

Carefree daytrippers captured by the camera of pioneer social realism photographer, Paul Martin, at Great Yarmouth around the turn of the century. At this time the one-day excursion remained for many people their only chance to visit the seaside each year

only to maintain the 'good' reputation of her house. In most boarding houses any 'hanky-panky' would, at this time, have been out of the question. But there were, in most seaside towns, poorer backstreet landladies who touted for custom at the railway stations as the holiday-makers arrived and who were probably quite happy to turn a blind eye to the revelries of their young guests. Some may have even encouraged them. Yet there can have been few young holiday-makers as fortunate as Bill Reed – a young postal worker at Mount Pleasant sorting office in London – in their choice of landlady.

> When we went on our holidays at Hastings, all the girls down there thought we were students. 'Cause we were, oh, you know, pretty well dressed and sort of confident of ourselves like. . . .Three of us decided to go to Hastings in 1914. We fixed up a place, a little pub called the Dripping Spring in Bohemia, Hastings, and it cost sixteen shillings a week full board. It was lovely, a great place it was. The lady, a great buxom woman, you know, liked young chaps I think, was amused with their talk and that, and she really made a fuss of us. Three of us went there, but there was ten others in the town all from Mount Pleasant, and all at different places. And we used to gather during the day, have a drink, and rowing and all that sort of thing, and about twice a week this lady at the pub she used to say, 'Fetch some of your boys up to tea.' So we'd say 'What, all ten of them?' 'Yes, that's all right, bring the ten up,' she says, 'bring 'em up to tea tonight.' And she was born locally at a village called Sattlestone. 'I'll get some girls from there,' so we used to have these girls in, you know. Had them all round the table there, a jolly good tea and then we used to get up in the room upstairs . . . and one of our chaps would get on the piano and used to have girls sing a song. There was a flat lead roof coming out in front and we'd get out there dancing, you know. Oh, a great time that was.

The briefness of most trips to the seaside must also have narrowed the opportunities for holiday dalliances, at least amongst working-class youth. Until the First World War the one-day excursion remained for many poorer people their only chance to visit the seaside each year. There were probably few prepared to risk the extra expense and parental disapproval involved in staying over for the night 'on spec' with girls they met – as did Jack Woolf, a Bolton labourer in the summer of 1907.

> Farnworth Co-op used to take us on half-day picnics every year. And this time we go to Blackpool, and dancing in Blackpool in the Tower, and with me is a friend called Simmons. Now he's only married like last week, do you see. So, train's due out at half-past ten. Twenty-five past ten I says, 'Hey, come on, else us be getting what'sname.' But no we had to stop with these two ladies. He said,

No. 7.   AUTUMN, 1904

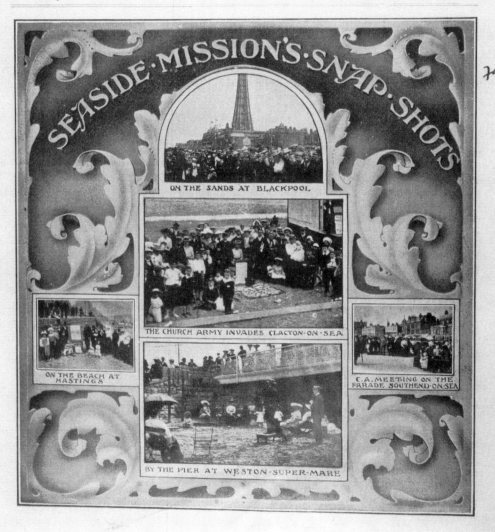

Seaside missions staged evening lectures as a counter attraction to what they saw as the dubious and dangerous night-time pleasures of holiday resorts

'I'm having these Lancers.' So I thought to myself, 'Well, you only got married last week, I've no ties.' I can stop. So we stopped. So these ladies come back ... we're in Blackpool now, these ladies went off home, so we're sleeping there and having our breakfast.

It was not until the inter-war years that a substantial number of young people began to enjoy a week's holiday by the sea independent of their parents. A gradual increase in wages, longer holidays – with pay for some young white-collar workers – and slightly more relaxed parental attitudes all played a part in this new trend. At the same time young people holidaying with their parents were often allowed a little more freedom than before the war. During Wakes' weeks, for example, gangs of young men and women who perhaps worked together might decide to stay in a different guest house or hotel to that of their parents. Added to this, the resorts, which by now had long established themselves as towns in their own right, had battalions of young seasonal workers as well as sizeable populations of young men and women many of whom seem to have been eager to join in the holiday fun.

A Church Army magazine celebrates its crusade to save souls at the seaside in the summer of 1904. In the first half of the century, seaside missions made special efforts to keep holidaymakers on the straight and narrow during a time of temptation

During the 1920s and 1930s the fun that popular seaside resorts like Blackpool promised young holiday-makers had a strong yet subtle sexual undercurrent. To begin with there were the publicity brochures and posters which often showed bathing beauties scantily dressed in the latest, briefest costumes. These 'pin-ups' reflected a real change in the atmosphere of seaside resorts after the war. The over-dressed Edwardian holiday-maker, who rarely bared an ankle or a knee or who hid from the sun under a boater or parasol, was now decidedly out of

A young couple stroll along Margate pier in 1905

date. The latest fashion was sunbathing, sun-lovers undressed on the beach and there was no question of sex segregation on the sands or bans on mixed bathing as there had been in many prudish resorts during the late Victorian and Edwardian times. The major resorts were entering a new phase of commercialization in which sexuality was seen as a selling point rather than a sin. Entertainment was increasingly geared to the growing demand amongst young people for exciting and glamorous places where they could meet, talk, drink and dance. The most popular attractions for the under-thirties were the modern dance halls where on most nights they could see the latest crooners and jazz bands. In this new era, 'letting your hair down' began to take on a different meaning and it is from this period that the stories of sexual misrule at the seaside really began to gain a hold on the popular imagination.

The sexual reputation of Blackpool was so great that in 1937 Mass Observation decided to investigate it. The broader aim of this group was an 'anthropological' study of everyday life in Britain by observing in minute detail 'ordinary' people's behaviour. During the summer of 1937 twenty-three observers armed with notepads and pencils began collecting information on holiday sex in Blackpool. They used a variety of methods, some of which required cunning and subterfuge. The observation of 'pick-ups' – boys meeting girls – was relatively easy as this frequently happened on promenades and beaches where observers could get a bird's-eye view whilst mingling unobserved in the passing crowds. Here is one observer's description of a beach scene on August Bank Holiday:

In one group one of the young men began betting one of the girls that she could not stand having smoke blown down her throat. She said she could, and knelt on the sand while he put his mouth over hers and blew some smoke into her face. She giggled and slithered down full length. This may have been accidental. The youth then held her down though she had made no attempt to rise, and continued to blow smoke in her face. Then he gave this up, and merely lay against her, and both became motionless. Then the friends who had been playing about on the sands came back. They did not seem surprised at seeing them sprawled on the sand, but as soon as they approached, the couple on the sand got up laughing and chafing, and began dusting themselves. Then the

Miss Modern magazine in August 1935. The inter-war years saw the glamorization of the seaside holiday as it became increasingly associated with sun worship and sexuality

girl's friend told the boy he was a bully to roughhouse with girls. The latter replied to this that if she didn't keep quiet he would do the same to her. Then a short scrap ensued in which all joined, the girls were easily overcome, and all ended up by more or less lying on each other in order to keep each other down. It ended by one of them getting up and proceeding to dress. Then they all got up and went off, one with his arm round the shoulder of one of the girls.

Because the beaches were so densely packed, observers were often able to position themselves a few yards away from amorous couples and note down their activities without arousing suspicion or rebuke. But sometimes a more devious approach was adopted by groups of observers.

Two couples on seats opposite the Palatine Hotel, facing the sea. We sat on seat adjacent, 20 yards south. TH commentated, RP screened him, HH wrote from the dictation, RG screened him, TIR pretended to be sick over the railings. . . . He snuggles up against her, she up to him, he down to her, her head goes away, his

'So this is Blackpool', a *Picture Post* snapshot in July 1939. By this time, Blackpool had acquired the reputation of being a kind of seaside sex capital

head follows, she accepts, they give one another the works. Time of kiss – 33 seconds. His head is up against her cheek, he is looking into her eyes. Her head goes right away. He scratches his nose with his right hand. He nuzzles into her, her head lies back. Time – 17 seconds.

Occasionally observers posed as 'pick-ups'. One young female observer described being chatted up by what she called a 'Jew boy':

He: What are you writing down?
Obs: Oh, I'm interested in gulls.
He: Is it the laundry?
Obs: No.
He: I should think you'd get a shirt for it if you sent it to the laundry. Had a good time last night.
Obs: Oh, where did you go?
He: I didn't get in till half-past two.
Obs: Well, where did you go?
He: I went to a strip-tease show.

'Sitting down and embracing.' This, according to Mass Observation in its seaside survey of 1937, was the most common kind of intimate behaviour on the beaches

Obs: Where was it at?

He: Why, are you interested in people getting undressed?

Obs: No, I'm interested in shows in Blackpool.

He: Well, if I told you you'd know as much as I do. Are you coming out with me tonight?

Obs: No.

He; You're a funny girl. (Pinches observer's cheek.) Well, I'll be going now.

The observers also compiled tantalizing surveys of intimate behaviour in Blackpool. On one evening between eleven thirty and midnight, they broke down the 232 cases of petting they had seen.

Sitting down and embracing – 120.
Standing up embracing – 42.
Lying on sand embracing – 46.
Sitting kissing – 25.
Necking in cars – 9.
Standing kissing – 3.
Girl sitting on man's knee – 7.

. . . so far we have seen only kissing, petting, necking. It will be noticed that the above table has no category for 'copulating'. There is a simple reason for this: none of these couples were copulating.

The observers went to extraordinary lengths to try to discover copulating couples.

When we began work in Blackpool we expected to see copulation everywhere. What we found was petting, feeling, masturbating one another. Observer units combed the sands at all hours, crawled around under the piers and hulkings, pretended to be drunk and fell in heaps on located sand couples to feel what they were doing exactly, while others hung over the seawall and railings for hours watching couples in their hollowed out sand-pits below. Lines of observers systematically beat the notorious sand dunes. . . . All the alleged sex areas were covered in this way, including 4 miles of prom, 2 miles of artificial cliff, 6 miles of sand, acres of dune and park. . . . Typical of the difference between truth and legend was an incident at one in the morning when a band of weary observers – weary from working the sands and dunes – stopped for coffee at an all-night stall on the prom. The stallholder, an old hand in Blackpool, in conversation said that it was disgusting the way some of the young people went on, that right now there were thousands on the sands, and a large part of them they'd stay there right through the night. In fact, there were three couples.

Despite this kind of exhaustive research over a period of several weeks only four cases of copulation were recorded – and one of these actually involved an observer. Mass Observation felt they had exploded the myth of casual sex in Blackpool – and by implication sex in other seaside resorts as well. Later they hit the headlines in the popular newspapers by describing Blackpool as 'the most moral town in England'.

Living memory, however, tells a different story which suggests that perhaps there was a lot going on at the seaside which Mass Observation's 1937 survey missed. Between 1935 and 1938 Walter Mack – then in his early twenties – spent most summer Saturdays looking for casual sex, often ending up on the Blackpool beaches with his partner for the night.

> There was no thought of courting or marrying these girls. No, I think I was quite mercenary about it, I wanted sex, I wanted a one-night stand and a lot of the girls wanted the same thing, they knew what they were doing. You'd go prepared, go to the barber's and get a Durex. But that was done to protect you not them. I was scared of getting VD. I remember I used to get the Durex and give them a little blow, put some air in them to make sure there was no holes in them. The place to go for the girls was the Winter Gardens or the Tower; you'd meet them there and if you liked the look of them you'd ask them for a dance. Dances finished at about half-past ten, eleven o'clock, so half an hour before the end you'd ask them out for a walk or something. Sometimes they wouldn't go down the steps on to the beach but often they didn't need much encouragement. And the favourite spot was near the Central Pier, between the North and Central piers, where there was softer dryer sand because the water didn't reach it so much. On that patch I'd say there were a dozen or twenty couples most summer evenings. And if it was raining you'd go under the pier. Well I'd pick a spot that was free and very often there'd be a couple making love say half a dozen yards away from where I was but nobody took any notice. You'd lie down, there'd be quite a lot of kissing and cuddling and the sex side of it was generally over quite quickly. I'm not saying I had what I wanted every time, perhaps it would be once a month, three out of every four attempts. Then after it was over I didn't waste any time, stand up, brush myself down, brush her down, we'd have a little chat. 'Where are you staying?' If she wasn't staying further away than the station I'd walk her to the steps of the boarding house. And that was it. I wouldn't see her again.

This kind of account of Blackpool night-life in the 1930s – which is not uncommon – really runs against the grain of Mass Observation's survey. Although their detailed reports give us a fascinating insight into the fantasy element in Blackpool's 'sexy' reputation, it seems to me they went too far the other way, portraying an equally misleading view of its chastity and sexual innocence. However, this was certainly not done deliberately. The observers were often young intellectuals, many of them Oxford undergraduates or graduates who probably had little experience or knowledge of outdoor sex of the type they were meant to be observing. From all accounts it was all over very fast, often within one or two minutes. And one of the fine arts of this kind of lovemaking was apparently secrecy: you covered yourself with a coat or embraced in such a way that it appeared there was nothing happening. In view of this it isn't very surprising that Mass Observation spotted so few copulating couples. Also many of the methods they used to try to detect sexual intercourse were, though ingenious, always likely just to produce evidence of 'petting'. One technique was to suddenly turn on head-lights in the dark backstreets favoured by young lovers. Car headlights were not very powerful in those days and to make things even more difficult 'standing-up sex' or 'the knee trembler' had the reputation of being very difficult to detect.

Mass Observation assumed that most of the secret sex going on in Blackpool would be amongst holiday-makers. My hunch though is that it was the casual seaside workers who really gave the holiday resorts their reputation for sexual misrule. Every summer most big holiday towns housed thousands of cooks, cleaners, washer-uppers, deck-chair attendants, stall holders, fairground assistants, actors, musicians and so on. Many were young and had probably left home to enjoy greater independence and freedom. Although they often worked long hours, in their free time they were subject to less supervision and control than almost any other young people in town. Betty White's mother often told the story of how she came to work in Blackpool in 1923:

> My mother lived in Burslem in the Potteries, her job was painting chinaware, but when she was nineteen she ran away from home. She used to say she couldn't stand it because my grandfather was an ex-sergeant-major in the army and he ruled with a rod of iron. And my mother's mother died when she was twelve and so because she was the eldest daughter her job was to look after all the family which was very hard because there was six children altogether. Anyway she came to Blackpool and worked as a skivvy in a boarding house. She was a very bonny girl, she won a competition as a harem girl at the Winter Gardens. Well, she had a respectable boyfriend but when she was twenty-one she got caught up with the glamour of the motor-bike addicts that roared into Blackpool from Barnsley every weekend. And she got preg-nant with me. She used to tell me that I was conceived under the North Pier. Disgusting isn't it, to think that that went on in those days. And she took the secret of who my father really was to the grave with her.

One group of seaside workers who quickly developed a reputation for sexual misconduct were those who staffed the early commercial holiday camps. The first Butlin's camps emerged in the late 1930s at Clacton and Skegness, and almost as soon as they had opened their doors there were allegations that, as Billy Butlin later put it, 'They were nothing more than hives of immorality.' The sexual legends of the early holiday camps rival those of Blackpool itself and there was very likely a similar fantasy element in both. Nevertheless, the fact that some staff – especially senior male staff – enjoyed their own private chalets provided a great opportunity for seaside sex which many probably took advantage of. Not all the girls, though, wanted to play ball. But if they refused they might be subjected to sexual violence and harassment by their young bosses. Odette Galley left home to begin work as a waitress in a south coast holiday camp in 1939 at the age of fifteen. To get the job she had lied and said she was eighteen:

Along with a group of girls, all considerably older, we were lined up for inspection like a cattle market, while Vic, the blond head waiter, scrutinized us. His eyes lit on me, and held, and I moved nervously from one foot to another. Although sexually aware, I was a virgin – a natural thing for young single girls in those days. We were set to work preparing the camp for visitors, cleaning, sewing endless curtains, humping furniture, stocktaking, checking china. Then one evening Vic summoned me to his chalet. The other girls exchanged knowing winks and nudges. 'Come in, love, sit here next to me. I won't bite.' 'Here' was the bed tucked against the wall and reluctantly I sat on the edge. 'That's better. Now, how are you liking it? Settled have you?' Before I could reply his arms clamped around me and then his mouth smothered mine and I was struggling to breath. He thrust my body backwards and covered it with his own. I started to scream. 'Stop it, you little bitch.' A slap to my face, another. He tore at my clothes and I screamed louder. Then as he raised himself to remove my panties, I gave an almighty heave and he toppled to the floor. 'You'll pay for this, you little cow.' I opened the door and ran. Finally exhausted I found myself out on the coast road and dropped on to the grass verge. I vomited violently. Eventually, after straightening my clothing, I crept back to the chalet. I could not tell anyone what had happened and was totally alone in my despair. Having to see him daily he did indeed make me pay, humiliating me on every possible occasion in front of the staff.

Far away from the big resorts and holiday camps a new kind of young day-tripper was emerging in the inter-war years who would add their names to the roll-call of lovers initiated into sex by the seaside. These were the countless thousands of young cyclists, motor cyclists and motorists who now enjoyed greater mobility than ever before because they could get to the coast under their own steam. They were lured by the romance of the sea and the sand, and the remote nooks and

Southend-on-Sea pier in 1948.
Many a holiday romance
blossomed on the pier, or on the
sands underneath it

Country-dancing at Butlin's holiday camp, Skegness, in 1939. Camps like this quickly developed a reputation for 'sexual immorality'

crannies far away from the madding crowd. Parents might be suspicious and only give their permission reluctantly. But nothing could be more innocent – so sons and daughters might plead – than a day out at the seaside.

Prior to the First World War many young people from poorer backgrounds had been unable to afford bicycles. By the 1930s mass production, cheaper prices and slightly better wages brought a bike within the grasp of practically all. A brand new Raleigh – the aristocrat of bikes – could be bought for under five pounds at this time and a second-hand bone-shaker picked up for just a few shillings. This was the great age of cycling on traffic-free country roads and in those days young people were happy to pedal long distances for a day out. A forty- or fifty-mile round trip to the coast would not put many off. In 1932 Ruby Parr was a nineteen-year-old domestic servant working in Toton, Hampshire. She remembers pedalling the twelve miles to Barton on Sea and back for her first taste of sex – which as with so many young women of her era proved to be a great disappointment.

> I worked for a nurse at Toton and she had a beach hut, and she used to lend me this when she wasn't using it herself at weekends. And I and this boy used to cycle down to this beach hut. . . . I never thought anything about going to this beach hut with this fellow. And we went inside and before we know where we are, we're lying on the bench. I can always, always remember my first

experience of sex. It was like a train going very fast. I don't remember that I was excited. Well, I never thought sex was that exciting. But again I never thought anything about it. I never thought, 'Oh, I shall end up with twins' or something or other like that, because you didn't know; you weren't told anything about that. All we were told was that we didn't do that sort of thing, but there were no consequences at the end of it, so it didn't worry me . . . and I'm a very curious person, I like to know the ins and outs of everything. It was more curiosity with me than anything. And quite frankly I was bored to tears.

While there were thought to be over ten million owners of bicycles in Britain in the 1930s, there were a further half a million motor cyclists. The new art of motor cycling was all the rage amongst young people during the inter-war years. Now on summer Sundays goggled couples might speed to the coast to enjoy a few hours together in a secluded spot – and perhaps make love – before returning for the ritual tea with parents. Lil Harvey was courting in Bristol in the early 1930s:

> Sometimes on a Sunday he used to borrow or pinch his brother's motor bike and sidecar and we used to go out in the country somewhere. We even used to go on the beach at Brean Down (and do it) in among the sand dunes, you know. Then I used to go back to his home for tea.

Some better-off young people who could afford cars also joined in this exodus to the coast on summer weekends. Amongst them was Lady Marguerite Tangye, then living away from home and working as a waitress in a London restaurant. She remembers her weekend jaunts on the south coast with her husband-to-be in the early 1930s:

> We used to go sailing and we would drive up from the boat, very tired and sleepy, get into a pub and say 'eggs and beans and sausages in bed on a tray'. And we'd go straight to bed at eight o'clock. And there would be sex and sausages and beans in bed. And we really enjoyed ourselves. It was absolutely gorgeous. We were mad about boats. And when you have something in common with somebody like that, if you've got a woman who is all right in night-clubs and is sophisticated in the week, and will rough it at the weekends, that's a man's ideal really. It was very rare. I was both. I was quite rare like that because I was a real rough it, adventurous person, I wouldn't mind where I was or how wet I was or what I did. And then, in the week, I could be at the top, sophisticated, photographed, and in every magazine. It was very suitable.

Some of these new day-trippers made for the big resorts where they were sometimes seen as a cause for concern. In Blackpool most alarm seems to have focused not on the early motor-cycle gangs who roared up and down the promenade, but on the rowdy coachloads of mill girls who arrived for Saturday night booze-ups. They were one of the targets of the Fylde House of Help, an organization run by local churches to stop girls who visited Blackpool from straying on to the path of temptation. Archdeacon Fosbrooke described 'young people who came from the Lancashire towns for the evening or the night in motor coaches' as a special problem.

> I have been told of as many as twenty or thirty young girls having to be dealt with in a state of intoxication. They come for a night out, they are not in the company of men. They take a glass of this and that, and being unaccustomed to it, and mixing it, they are very often in a pitiable condition before the night is out. . . . They were obviously in danger of any suggestion that might be made to them.

Another new tradition which was to further enhance the sexual mystique of the seaside resort was that of courting couples spending a holiday together. In late Victorian times this kind of thing was almost unheard of, but by the inter-war years an increasing number of couples – often engaged or shortly to be married – seem to have persuaded their parents to let them go away by themselves. Their consent, though, was usually accompanied by dire warnings of the consequences should there be any trouble and an insistence that they should sleep in separate rooms.

In their study of Blackpool, Mass Observation's intrepid investigators exposed all the most obvious boarding house myths – that there were secret doors and secret affairs going on between strangers – but they seem to have ignored this important new trend in courtship. When a young couple arrived they might – as in the popular seaside joke – book a double bedroom on the pretence that they were married and go to the trouble of wearing 'fake' wedding rings to prove it. More often, though, they would book separate single rooms in the boarding house or hotel, perhaps mentioning that they were engaged. No doubt there were still landladies, some of whom were fighting a rearguard action to maintain the moral purity of their towns, who would strongly disapprove of such arrangements. But by the inter-war years many seem to have become more interested in young holiday-makers' money than their morals – none of my interviewees were refused accommodation on the grounds that they were not married. Once established in the house or hotel there was often no shortage of opportunities to 'visit' or be alone in each other's room. In 1932 Jack Baker, a footman in his late twenties, went away with his fiancée, whom he had been courting for three years.

> We went on holiday at Bognor, to a nice boarding house. We were away for a fortnight and we had separate rooms. But of course there were no tin tacks on the floor in the passage so it was quite

Courting couples on Blackpool beach in the 1930s. A new trend in the inter-war years was to go away for a week's holiday together – partly, though this was kept secret, to get some sexual experience

easy to go from one room to the other, and we used to call on each other. It was quite free, you were left alone, you were visitors, you see, and what you did was your own business, as it is today I would assume.

In 1937 Gwen Taylor persuaded her mother – behind her father's back – to let her go away on holiday with her husband-to-be. They aroused a great deal of curiosity amongst the other guests in the boarding house where they stayed, which was probably not unconnected to the fact that Gwen was a very young looking seventeen year old and her boyfriend was ten years older.

My boyfriend, as he'd become then, said 'Well, would you like to come down to New Malden to my parents' and we'll go off down to Ramsgate.' So I argued with my mother for a little bit, but she was all right and she said, 'For goodness sake as long as you're back before your father comes back out of hospital.' So yes, we went, and his mother didn't like the idea very much but anyhow we went off down to Ramsgate. And we found a bed and breakfast place and asked for two rooms. Well, there wasn't two rooms but the landlady agreed I could have a bedroom and she would put us a bed up for my husband-to-be in the dining room and take it down in the morning. But the romance had got such then that we were more intimate. So he used to ruffle his bed up at night and creep up the stairs, then rush down in the morning and be packing his bed up ready for landlady to put it up. This went on and we used to go down to breakfast and there used to be the other guests who were very curious, you know, you could see them giving glances. Then we used to go off for the day. And when you walked out of the gate in the morning all the guests were at the window – it was one of those Victorian houses with a bay window – there were all faces at the window. And you walked up the road thinking 'oh love,' you felt you were undressed or something, it was awful. But I think they were amused more than anything, I think it caused a bit of excitement.

If staid seaside visitors imagined that fun-loving sexual romps were going on under their very noses they were very far from the truth. Seaside sex was probably for most young couples as awkward, guilt-ridden and frightening – at least for the young woman – as any other sort of sex before marriage at this time. To have sex, possibly for the first time, in a room where you were far away from parents and likely to be undisturbed, was indeed one of the main attractions for courting couples going on holiday together. But equally important was the desire to spend more time alone together with no parental interference, just to see if you got on. The seaside holiday was the closest most couples probably got to 'living together' or a 'trial marriage', even though it all took place in a very idyllic setting. Gwen Taylor:

Half the idea of it was to spend the night together, it was the next thing to marriage. . . . But before that we only saw each other one evening a week and then probably every other Sunday afternoon or evening. And it isn't enough in two years' courtship really. So I think, by going on holiday, we were together for a week. It was only a week, but we spent all day together. We didn't have much money, in fact I think the money ran out towards the end of the week. . . . But the holiday was really nice because we felt like just a couple with nobody else. It was our business and our affair and there was nobody else around to watch you or ask you questions, 'Oh don't do that' or anything else. And so it was just us for a holiday. We'd sit on the beach, sunbathe and go into the sea.

One of the few ways we can begin to gauge how much sex was going on at the seaside, with hard statistics, is by looking at birth-rates. There was a long tradition in Britain (as in most other countries) for more babies to be conceived during the summer months than at any other time of the year. This fits – or certainly doesn't contradict – the idea that seaside sex was important but it doesn't really shed much light on what was happening, when, with whom and where. One intriguing thing to do, which would be another research project in itself, would be to see if the birth-rates, especially the illegitimacy rates, in northern industrial towns peaked nine months after their Wakes' week. Time has prevented me from doing this but I have looked at the illegitimacy rates for English seaside towns and they make intriguing reading. Until the First World War they hovered around the national average of 4 to 5 per cent, sometimes a little above but nothing spectacular. During the inter-war years, however, they surged upwards. Blackpool found itself with one of the highest illegitimacy rates in England. In some years, for example 1922 and 1928, it spiralled to ten per cent, and in many others it was around the 8 per cent mark – about twice the national average. Many of these babies were conceived during the holiday season.

But we can only guess who the young mothers were. There are few records of where they came from and what they did. To make things more difficult there seems to have often been a conspiracy of silence to cover up what was seen as an embarrassing blot on a resort's reputation. The earliest comment I have found by any Medical Officer of Health or medical authority for Blackpool on the town's extraordinarily high illegitimacy rate came in March 1959. A reporter from the *Evening Gazette* was told that: 'Figures issued by the Ministry of Health which placed Blackpool's percentage of illegitimate births the highest in the country probably bear no reflection on the town's resident population, according to a leading local medical authority. Blackpool, he said, has always had a fairly high number of illegitimate births. While it was difficult to know the exact reason, one explanation was that many girls expecting illegitimate children came to Blackpool to have them, away from their home towns. "They seem to think that people are more broad-minded here," he added. "Whether they are or not I wouldn't know."'

This explanation probably has a small grain of truth in it. Some nursing homes for the elderly in seaside towns did occasionally make arrangements wit' well-to-do parents who wanted a disgraced daughter to have her illegitimate baby well away from home. Some Blackpool landladies also remember that very occasionally pregnant girls would arrive looking for jobs as skivvies or maids in the town's many boarding houses and hotels. They were probably lured by the legend of Blackpool's free and easy attitude to sex, and perhaps used to spend their holidays there. But if they thought they might receive more sympathetic treatment they were in for a nasty shock. For before the Second World War Blackpool's Public Assistance department rigorously applied the 'settlement' regulations whereby an unmarried mother was technically not entitled to any help unless she had lived and worked in the town for at least twelve months. If there had been any mass migration of pregnant girls hoping for assistance in Blackpool they would have quickly been sent back to their home towns. An added disincentive to stay was the fact that the local Conservative council was notorious for harbouring one of the most antiquated systems of ante-natal care in the country. The most likely explanation for the high illegitimacy rates in resorts like Blackpool is that most of the children were born to young women who lived and worked locally. Many were probably casual workers who had left home to work in the seaside industries. Others were local girls who had casual affairs or holiday romances with the droves of young men who arrived each summer in the big resorts.

During the war many big resorts were taken over as billets for the armed forces or evacuees, while other smaller seaside towns became 'bolt holes' for middle-class women escaping from civilian bombing. By the mid-1950s, however, the sexual traditions that first emerged during the early part of the century surfaced again to be invigorated by higher wages, paid holidays and the greater freedom and independence of young people. For the next ten years seaside sex reached its zenith as millions of young people flooded to commercialized stretches of coast-line all over Britain. The illegitimacy rates in the seaside towns continued to climb upwards and resorts like Blackpool, Brighton and Bournemouth won the unenviable reputation of always being near the top of the illegitimacy league table. But by the late 1960s the saucy seaside holiday was beginning to fall prey to the new 'more permissive' age. It appeared rather seedy and old-fashioned. More and more young people rented flats of their own or lived together openly if they were so inclined – they did not have to scuttle off to the coast for secret sex as did previous generations. And in the new era of international air travel and cheap package holidays, many looked further afield for romance, adventure and sex – to what Laurie Taylor has called the 'Costa del Hanky Panky'. The sexual legends of Benidorm soon eclipsed those of Blackpool.

8

THE OTHER LOVE

In the late 1940s Dudley Cave, then a young cinema manager who was homosexual, did not know of the few gay bars that existed in the capital. He sought like-minded young men wherever he could and that included public lavatories.

> In some lavatories there would be quite a small hole, big enough to peer through but too small for anything else. If the person on the other side looked interested and interesting there could be an exchange of notes. These notes usually asked, 'Have you any-where to go?' as often people had wives at home and it would be pointless to meet just for a cup of coffee and a chat. On the other hand the reply could be: 'My flat's ten minutes away'. . . . It was all very anonymous, names were rarely exchanged and most people covered the number on their phone if they were hoping to bring someone back. Sometimes these encounters developed into stable loving relationships. But couples who met this way would often pretend they had met at a party because picking up men in this way was looked down upon.

This practice of picking up homosexual men in public toilets – usually for casual sex – was and still is known as cottaging. A cottage is the name given to the stall or lavatory used for pick-ups – this is how the term seems to have derived. Cottaging was surrounded with secrecy and subterfuge because toilets were periodically raided by the police and *agents provocateurs* were planted to arrest those who were soliciting. Despite the secrecy most young homosexuals had a clear idea of what class of person they would be likely to meet in particular toilets. But whereas in conventional society the classes were very much divided, in the cottage there was the desire to have sexual experience with men from all walks of life. Bernard Williams, then a young schoolteacher, also remembers cottaging in the capital just after the Second World War:

> If you wanted a piece of rough you'd look around the cottages in Covent Garden, in the early morning cottages, the lorry drivers' cottages. On the other hand if you wanted the theatrical trade you'd do some of the cottages round the back of Jermyn Street or if you did the cottage at Waterloo Station you always got a good class of trade there, dear. It was just what you were looking for, I suppose. My style was very much sort of looking someone up and

down, them looking me up and down, umm yes, you are me, dear, or I hope I'm you, you know the sort of thing I mean. Your mind worked at the speed of knots. You wandered into a cottage, and if you saw somebody that you liked you'd stand within looking distance possibly. If you'd got any wits about you you'd click and wander off somewhere. The risks were enormous because I mean you could have been picked up by the police, or you could have been picked up by a thug and your career gone for a burton.

Between the 1890s and the late 1950s most homosexuals were forced to inhabit a twilight world beyond the pale of respectable society. This period was marked by new legal controls policing and punishing homosexuality, and a deep public revulsion against this kind of sexual relationship. The Social Purity Movement in part initiated this hostility, attacking homosexuality as a corrupter of youth, the family and the British Empire. From late Victorian times onwards the term homosexual gained wide currency as a person different and inferior to other men. Prior to this they had been called sodomites which had a much more bi-sexual association – these were men with an occasional taste for buggery. But increasingly homosexuals and lesbians – whose stigmatization came slightly later in the 1920s – were fixed in the public mind as folk devils. Mass Observation's sex survey of 1949 claimed that most British people were horrified and disgusted by homosexuality. As one 48-year-old coal depot manager put it, 'I shouldn't think they're human. . . . I mean animals don't do that I shouldn't think.' This level of ignorance and prejudice had a profound impact on the young homosexual. So, too, did the emerging idea that they were a separate species. This chapter tells the story of some of the young homosexual men and women of this period, and of the secret world they inhabited.

Ironically the late Victorian obsession with keeping boys and girls apart during their 'impressionable years' greatly encouraged homosexual relationships, if only transient ones. This tradition of encouraging boys and girls and young men and women to inhabit separate spheres – at school, at work, in the street, in youth organizations and sometimes at home – was to remain very important until the 1950s. The consequence was that the closest and most intimate relationships that they formed were with members of their own sex. Sometimes there was a physical side to this relationship. The first strongly homosexual experiences of those I have interviewed generally occurred during the teenage years. But most didn't define these experiences as homosexual or worry that they were not what they had come to think of as 'normal'.

Sometimes these homosexual relationships began at home. Bedrooms or – in overcrowded working-class homes – beds, would be shared by brothers or sisters. We will never know how many incestuous relationships developed as a result of this. But some social reformers around the turn of the century thought this was a serious problem and the moral dangers of overcrowding and of shared beds became a major

Public lavatories were one of the main meeting places for young homosexuals before the war

plank in subsequent campaigns for housing reform. The most appalling overcrowding actually occurred not in homes but in poor lodging
and boarding houses for casual labourers who moved from place to
place in their work. These, too, were becoming increasingly sex
segregated as a result of the campaigns of moral reformers. Billy
MacNiel, born in 1915, was brought up by his mother and grandmother who ran a cheap boarding or 'bob' house near Banff in
north-east Scotland:

> My gran and mother ran a bob house for many years, mostly for
> long-distance drivers and their mates, who were mostly young
> lads. Gran charged two and sixpence nightly and slept them
> mostly two to three in double beds and often if we were full up I
> was joined by one or two sleeping with me, mostly young lads. At
> this time I would have been ten or eleven years old, very green and
> I knew little about sex. So that when these boys snuggled me, for a
> long time I didn't associate it with anything sexual and my ma
> often accused me of bed-wetting. But I was made aware of what
> was really happening to me when on a nightshift one of these
> young lads had a bit more to drink and his driver got stewed. The
> boy was put in with me and he was legless. But he must have
> woken up about an hour after we went to sleep and been feeling
> randy. I became aware that his hands were all over my body. He'd
> taken off my pants and vest and was rolling me on to my front and
> trying to get his cock up my arse. I didn't know it was his cock. I
> thought it was his fingers. But the pain was real and I was
> conscious for the first time that I had a rock – it was erected. I
> remember the shame I felt and at the same time wanted it to go
> on. . . . Was that the start of my queerness? I think so.

A single homosexual act seldom had the power to change sexual
preferences and reform a sexual identity as seems to have occurred
with Billy MacNiel. According to most people I have spoken to, actual
intercourse was quite rare among young teenagers. Much more common was mutual masturbation. Most of those who practised this seem
to have gone on to have been strongly heterosexual. This was encouraged by the fact that the popular homosexual practice of mutual
masturbation had macho associations amongst many young teenage
boys. One of the main considerations which made this habit so popular
was that most boys did not meet many girls and even then there was
little chance of any sexual contact. Ray Rochford:

> Around the age of thirteen or fourteen I can vividly recall one hot
> Sunday afternoon, lying in the long grass on the side of the canal
> with my friends. Tommy Race, the oldest one, began boasting
> about what he had done to this girl who lodged with his parents.
> As he expounded on the different positions that he had made her
> assume – all nonsense of course – we all got a hard-on. . . . As one

The popular homosexual practice of mutual masturbation was widely practised among boys. For them it had macho heterosexual associations

we all brought out our erections and quite instinctively we masturbated the lad nearest to us. I wanked Frank and he wanked me for the simple reason it was more pleasurable from someone else's hand. After all seven of us had ejaculated we dozed off in that hot summer sun of 1936. This was a very common occurrence and we never felt any shame whatsoever. We never for one second thought that what we were actually doing was participating in homosexual practices. We didn't even know what the word homosexual meant. We had never read it or heard of it. To us it was a perfectly normal and natural thing to do, and it was quite common amongst gangs of lads. If you could by any stretch of the imagination get a female to do it, all the better, but I'm afraid that was right out of the question. No way.

Mutual masturbation also had a popular macho image amongst middle-class youth and in grammar and public schools. Dudley Cave went to Haberdashers' Aske's school in London during the 1930s.

At our school sexual play between boys was quite common, in fact after football we would go into a flooded room for a bath and the bathing was supervised by a master standing on the steps. And he could see the boys on the left-hand side of the bath but the boys

Dudley Cave, aged thirteen, on holiday with his mother in the 1930s

on the right-hand side were tucked out of sight. And those we regarded as cissies would stay on the left under the watchful eye of the master, while the real men would be playing with each other on the other side out of sight. The attitude was very much that we were the real guys and they were the cissies.

Schoolboy homosexuality had long been institutionalized in British boarding schools, mainly because the pupils lived in and there was little or no opportunity for contact with girls between the ages of about thirteen to eighteen. But the boom in single sex public schools from Victorian times onwards made these traditions much more important. Indeed homosexuality among middle-class boys became so common that the conventional wisdom of adult authority was that of a temporary period of homosexual attachment was a natural stage in the growing-up process. In his social history, *The Public School Phenomenon* (1977), Jonathan Gathorne-Hardy estimated that around a quarter of all pupils had a regular sexual relationship. Many more had occasional sex or romantic adventures with other boys. Love letters were frequently passed amongst pupils and at some schools like Wellington in the 1930s, homosexuality was so fashionable that pretty young boys were virtually raped. This kind of atmosphere attracted schoolmasters with homosexual leanings, but though they might turn a blind eye to some of their pupils' practices, few dared to encourage homosexuality or have affairs with them. With the growing hostility towards homosexuality, cases of this kind provoked public outrage and few teachers risked ruining their careers. John Summerhays went to a minor public school during the early years of the Second World War:

> There was considerable sexual activity in the dormitories, though I don't think that there was ever anything more adventurous than mutual masturbation. Of that, however, there was plenty, and it was normal practice for boys to spend nights together. At first I would have nothing to do with this, and kept away from the activity, but later joined in and enjoyed myself. There may have been some screwing going on among older boys, but I think I would have heard of it. I know that it was some time after I left school that I became aware it was possible for men to screw together. Occasionally a master would make a tour of the dormitories late at night, and would find about one third of the beds empty. By coincidence, another third were each occupied by two. This was not regarded as a great crime, and I do not think it was thought of as real or serious homosexuality. Standard punishment was a lecture and six strokes with the cane. We became word perfect on the lecture. I think that had anything more been going on there would have been a row.

In the new public and private schools for the girls of the well-to-do there emerged a parallel tradition of lesbianism. It was most noticeable

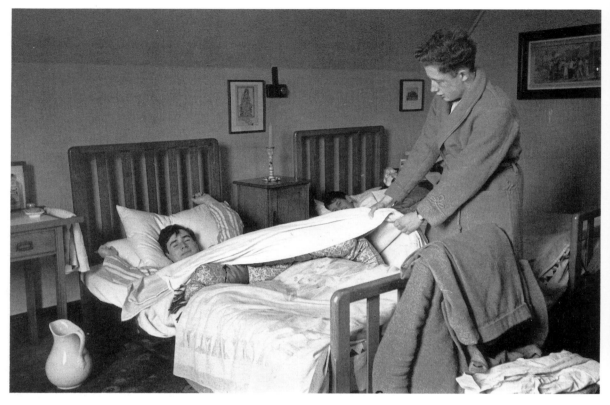

amongst pupils aged between eleven and fifteen, when the love for an older girl, often referred to as a 'crush', a 'pash' or a 'rave', was common. After this most girls developed heterosexual interests and fantasies – not infrequently for new film stars. But the isolated existence in schools like Rodean and Calne, and the ban on contact with boys, encouraged same sex passions into the mid teens and these often focused on the young schoolmistress.

How far these relationships were physical is impossible to know. My hunch is that most often they were not. They probably remained on a level of emotional lesbianism. Perhaps most common was an intense love – at a distance – for prefects, lacrosse players and dancing teachers, of the sort portrayed by Angela Brazil in her best-selling novels about girls' schools during the inter-war years. But there is little doubt that there were some sexual relationships between girls. In the 1920s, a decade when the term lesbian first really entered into public debate, with the banning of Radclyffe Hall's lesbian novel *The Well of Loneliness*, some headmistresses at places like Clapham High School and Cheltenham Ladies College began issuing regular warnings and lectures on the moral dangers of crushes.

Some of the affairs, however, were allegedly initiated by the staff themselves. It is likely that some of the teachers were lesbians – a career

Public schoolboys at Shrewsbury in 1940. Homosexuality had long been institutionalized in boarding schools

in a girls' school must have been an attractive prospect for women who were happiest amongst their own sex. In 1922, in a book called *The Psychology of Mis-conduct, Vice and Crime*, Bernard Hollander attacked lesbian teachers: 'Unsuspecting parents are little aware of how common homosexuality is among women, and how many little girls get seduced to the practice.' He claimed to know of one school which was closed down because of 'the degrading and criminal habits of the head mistress who for years had seduced one girl after another'. Marie Stopes was also a powerful campaigner against lesbian teachers in the inter-war years, partly perhaps because she had been unhappy after

Front cover of a book by Angela Brazil, the popular novelist who wrote about life in girls' schools. Her most avid readers were adolescent females. Many of her stories portray a subconscious emotional lesbianism which was probably quite common in these schools

falling passionately in love with one of her teachers twenty-five years before. I have found it impossible to track down any teachers or former boarding school pupils who are now lesbians to give their point of view. Of those heterosexual women I have spoken to who went to these schools, most felt that the lesbian crushes of their early teens were in a sense manufactured by the single sex institutions they found themselves in. Lady Marguerite Tangye was sent to a girls' boarding school in the mid-1920s:

> I did get the odd pashes on the athletic girls a bit. It showed really that I was thoroughly normal. Up to thirteen I liked boys and then when I was sent to the girls' school, because it was one sex only, I did rather admire the athletic girls. So it shows boarding schools are pernicious like that. . . . There were three girls expelled, my mother told me, for lesbian activities. She was fascinated by this, I wasn't at all. I think one was a cousin of mine but I wasn't really interested.

Single sex relationships continued at university colleges, most of which were sex segregated, catering mainly for men. Homosexuality was very fashionable at inter-war Oxbridge. For some it was tied up with rebellion against the growing prejudice against homosexuality outside the universities. But the dramatic increase in single sex college and boarding school education from Victorian times onwards did not lead to a dramatic increase in the homosexual inclinations in the adult population. For when they left this cloistered student world most young people left behind their homosexual past and looked forward to a heterosexual future. They were now subject to a new set of pressures – most of all to get engaged and married – and they began to enjoy opportunities for loving relationships with members of the opposite sex which had previously been denied. Outside public schools and colleges, homosexuality was very much taboo. This taboo seems to have been increasingly shared by all classes of society. John Binns, an apprentice printer in London in the 1930s, remembers the hostile attitudes towards homosexuals amongst working people at this time:

> We very seldom had contact with homosexuals and when we did we treated them as a joke. We had various names for them, not very nice names. If we wanted to describe a gay man with a gay man we used to say, 'He's pushing shit up hill', that used to be a phrase. I think pansies used to be used, but not very much, and the real word we used was 'brown hatters'. And I think in cockney language that summed it all up. . . . Gays, they've got status now, but they never used to before. I just used to class it as buggery, just couldn't stand it.

This growing taboo on homosexuality was not embraced by all working-class people. There were long traditions of homosexuality in the army and the navy – arising in many cases from the absence of

The knobbly knees competition at Butlin's holiday camp, Skegness, in 1939, provides an opportunity to parody the mincing walk of the popular stereotype homosexual

women – and here there remained a greater tolerance of it and a greater interest in sexual experimentation. Homosexuality also seems to have been not uncommon among working-class youth in late Victorian and Edwardian times. A number of trials around the turn of the century, such as the one involving Oscar Wilde, illustrated how there was then no shortage of stable lads, newspaper sellers and the like, prepared to sell their bodies for money. Poverty provided a strong incentive for young men to get involved in casual prostitution. Rent boys were certainly not unknown in Edwardian times. But the spread of state schooling, the influence of moral crusades aimed at youth, and gradual improvements in the standard of living made this kind of trade quite rare by the inter-war years. My interviews suggest that by then many young working people seem to have adopted a very respectable rejection of homosexuality.

Those who broke these taboos often had a torrid time. Many desperately hoped that they would grow out of the homosexuality that was enshrined in the public school way of life. When they did not they were usually very worried. The roughest ride faced young homosexuals who left privileged all-male schools to enter a working-class environment. There was often immense hostility towards homosexuals especially in the work-place, and when this was combined with class antagonism towards someone from a superior background, it might spill over into harassment and violence. John Summerhays left public school at the age of fifteen in 1946 to begin work as a 'boy' at a small engineering works in South London:

> My background, dress, accent and opinions did not endear me to my workmates, and I had a fairly rough time at first. I went through the usual initiation ceremony administered by the girls in the shop – this involved a milk bottle and spiders and this upset me. However, after a time I did become accepted, partly because among the boys I was the only one who could read and write properly. During the war the others had all been evacuated to villages in North Wales, and had had virtually no education during those years. It was during this time that I began to realize that my fellows' tastes were not the same as my own. I was the only one of my age who did not screw a girl at every opportunity. This lack of appetite was attributed charitably to my middle-class background, it being generally believed that I 'didn't know what it was for'. However, when invited on blind dates I did not do well. I did feel under pressure to go out on occasions with one or another of the girls and received careful and tender instruction in shop doorways and backstreet arches on the purpose and use of my equipment. I did lose my virginity but although I enjoyed their company I found the physical side unpleasant with a woman. I did not enjoy the sexual experience and really did not see what all the fuss was about. I preferred masturbation, though I was by now

having to do this alone and was lonely. My fantasies were almost entirely about men, often involving the lads at work. I very badly wanted a man to sleep with, but this was out of the question.

A brief homosexual relationship with a young man on a course he attended gave John enough confidence to reveal to his best friend at work that he was gay:

When I returned south in December 1948 I decided to tell my mate with whom I lodged of my homosexuality and to my astonishment and relief he accepted it as something to which I had a right. However, he did not keep it to himself, and some of the others did give me a bad time. I was beaten up several times and various unpleasant tricks were played on me. There was quite a lot of rough treatment including some hair-raising experiments. Some of the blatantly heterosexual young men were the most scornful of me as a 'queer' and turned out to be pretty nasty and revealed some unexpected interests. A factory workshop is full of all sorts of equipment. If some of the other lads had not been good-hearted I would have been very seriously maimed or killed by these attentions. At the time I was living in terror and despair and totally isolated. . . . Homosexuality, blackmail and assault were all illegal, but I would not have had much help if I'd gone to the police for protection against my workmates.

Homosexual young men who entered a professional or managerial career were often spared the daily threat of harassment and violence. Instead they had to contend with the likelihood of instant dismissal should their sexuality be detected. After being de-mobbed in 1945 Dudley Cave became a cinema manager in North London:

I did have sex with people at work, never imposing on them. And when it subsequently became rumoured that I was gay, my district manager got to hear about it, asked me, and I couldn't or didn't deny it. I was suspended and hauled up to Head Office and they decided I should go. In fact he suggested I might like to resign and I, thank goodness, said 'no', I didn't feel like that. I eventually left Odeon theatres with three months pay in lieu of notice. I felt absolutely dreadful about it. I felt dreadful because I had to tell my father I had been sacked or was leaving, without telling him the reason. I felt totally friendless and alone and very demoralized.

Most young homosexuals were too frightened to be open about their sexuality so they led a double life, meeting each other secretly in well-known haunts, often at night. Many larger towns and cities would have a few pubs or possibly clubs known to be inhabited by homosexuals or lesbians, and swimming or vapour baths also proved popular as meeting places. Young lesbians in London just after the Second World War met at a handful of 'ladies' clubs', notably 'The Gateway', a

Bow swimming baths, East London, around the turn of the century. Swimming baths – along with public lavatories – became popular meeting places for young homosexuals

few selected Lyons Corner Houses, and at friends' homes. But homosexuality was so taboo that those who were too public about their sexual tastes ran the risk of attracting dangerous rumours and black-mailers. Since homosexuality was illegal, there was also the possibility of arrest which might result in the ruin of a young man's career and his being disowned by his family. To avoid detection semi-dark and subterranean meeting places were far and away the most popular, at least amongst homosexual young men – we know far less about the lesbian meeting places and relationships. Packed picture palaces, cinemas and music halls were favourite spots for soliciting. Sometimes groups of homosexuals made inadvertent – or perhaps deliberate – sexual advances to heterosexual young men. John Binns remembers going to the Islington Music Hall in North London in the early 1930s:

> If all the seats were taken they allowed you to stand for a reduced price in the gallery. And I shot up there and I was enjoying this turn and all of a sudden someone undone me bloody flies and started pulling me off. Much to my discredit I let them do it for a couple of minutes before I buzzed off and I thought, 'Oh blimey'. It was the biggest shock of my life that kind of thing. I never liked them [homosexuals] for a start, but to do that to me. So I shot off into another part of the gallery. And what I can see of it is that

there was a mob that got together and probably done it to everybody. While they were doing it to me someone pushed themselves up against my back and expected me to do it to them.

One well-known landmark for London homosexuals was Epping Forest. Paul Lanning, born in a mining village near Chester in 1905, arrived in London in the early 1930s to become a school teacher:

I had a flat near Epping Forest and that used to be the haunt of London. I used to go to the forest, take walks in the forest and there were just chaps walking around. It was pretty ugly but there was no alternative. Epping Forest was full and the police cars would come through and they would all be chased away like butterflys. . . . It was a shocking place. Roman orgies were there. Epping Forest was notorious, it was ugly in the extreme. And you were always discontented when you left the place, always ashamed of yourself. Everything happened there. Trousers up, cocks down, cocks in, horrible. I went through all that. Masturbation, sodomy, sucking, it was all there, and I knew the whole lot in that place. And it was very very risky, absolutely promiscuous. . . . My chief achievement was a police sergeant of Leytonstone Police Station. I was caught taking somebody home at two o'clock in the morning – and we were always suspect if we were out late in Epping Forest – and he came to me and asked me for my address, 'Where do you live?' I said, 'I live over there, I'm a local man.' And he said, 'Right, sir,' and the next time he saw me in the street he spoke to me and said that although he represented the law he was a private citizen and did what he liked. The old rascal. I didn't invite him back to my place, he came. Oh that's a triumph, that's anybody's triumph to have the police sergeant.

Most popular of all meeting places were public urinals and lavatories. The late Victorian and Edwardian conveniences, often fashioned out of iron with latticework design, proved to be perfect settings for cottaging. Those inside could spy on each other through the stalls and make sexual advances while at the same time keeping a look out for anyone approaching outside. One of the most well known of these urinals was 'Clerkson's Cottage' in Dansey Place, off Wardour Street in the West End of London. The larger public lavatories, for example in bus and railway stations which had toilets as well as urinals, were also favourite haunts. Appointments for sexual adventures could be made using graffiti on the walls. But most involved in this 'trade', however, had more subtle techniques. Paul Lanning:

We had all these public conveniences around, the one in Notting Hill Gate was one of the well-known places. You'd just stand in the stall and smile and wait outside and see what happened. We had our techniques, you know, we'd walk outside, just hang around. For example, my black friend who was a very fine chap, an educated man, I met him in the Tottenham Court Road place and I went outside, looked in a book shop. Our technique was that he came and looked at the book shop, and say 'How do you do, what are you doing?' and so it was so easy if you knew your techniques.

The police usually seem to have turned a blind eye to this secret homosexual culture. But from time to time there were purges on a local or national scale, usually in response to some moral panic. The most zealous clean-up campaign occurred in the early 1950s and was partly triggered by the close links between secret homosexuality and the Guy Burgess spy scandal. In 1952 prosecutions for sodomy, gross indecency and importuning spiralled to about five times the 1938 level – though in 1952 there were still only 670 cases of sodomy known to the police. One technique used by the police was planting an attractive *agent provocateur* in the toilets. Paul Lanning remembers how he was almost trapped by this method one evening when he came out of a well-known public convenience in the Strand in the late 1930s:

I was approached by a man in the street, 'Hello, where have you been to?' that kind of thing, an ordinary conversation. And he pummelled me until he got my texture, and he was a nasty piece of work, and he said, 'Let's go home and have a drink.' I went to have a drink with him up the Strand and then when he was all very pleasant, he showed me a lapel, he was an inspector. He said 'Now you come with me to Marylebone Police Station.' Luckily I was acute. To my surprise he paid the drink bill and when he was paying it I gave him the slip. Naturally I ran down the Strand. I had legs then.

Most of the encounters which occurred in these clandestine meeting places seem to have been furtive and concerned primarily with casual sex. The element of danger probably added to the excitement of it all. Some lasting relationships did grow out of fleeting lavatory loves but most common was the one-night stand – sometimes culminating in sex in the lavatory itself. This kind of sexual relationship fitted in neatly with the double life that homosexuals were forced to lead at the time. Many of those cottaging would have had a girlfriend or perhaps even a wife. And the prejudice and hostility towards homosexuality made it difficult for young men outside more liberal literary and theatrical circles to live together in a permanent relationship. Deprived for the most part of long-term loving relationships many of those who were caught up in cottaging felt a deep sense of dissatisfaction and unhappiness. Bernard Williams regularly toured the capital's cottages in the late 1940s:

It was very common for somebody to toss someone off in a cottage. One did. I don't think I ever did anything but toss somebody off and be tossed off in a cottage. But I mean certainly I

An Edwardian lesbian postcard with a classical flavour

411/2

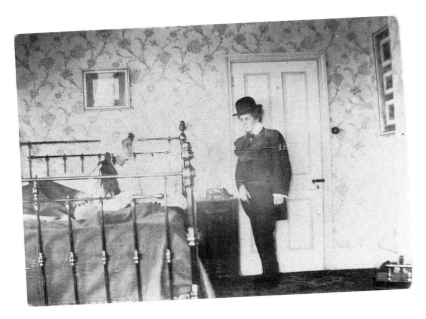

A rare lesbian postcard. This one was sent from Leighton Buzzard to Miss Brook in Camberley, Surrey, in 1906. The intriguing message on the back reads: 'Do you notice where my boots are?', suggesting that the card might have been sent by one of the women in the photograph

have gone into cottages and seen guys being screwed. If, because of the pressures of society, you are unable to make any satisfactory relationship with somebody, inevitably most people want sex, and so if the only contacts you make are casual ones in cottages, it's only a temporary satisfaction. There was no emotional thing in it. You were driven on, one to another to another to another.

The isolation and guilt experienced by most homosexuals, together with the enormous pressures to conform, pushed many into a hetero-sexual marriage. Many more young homosexuals and lesbians married before the 1950s than today when they have a much more established culture and social identity. Some, especially young men, hoped that marriage might 'cure' them of their 'abnormal' desires. Others, especially young women, entered marriage only dimly aware of the possibility that they might be lesbians. This was primarily because lesbianism was much more hidden from public view than homosexuality. In June 1939 Sharley McLaine, a Jewish refugee from Germany, escaped to London, fleeing from the concentration camps where both of her parents were to die. Only half-aware of her lesbianism she married – a conscientious objector – in 1944, partly to avoid zenophobic hostility and to obtain British nationality:

I had one very, very good friend and we were friends since very early childhood and I can remember at the age of twelve or thirteen, when she had a boyfriend, I couldn't understand why she should prefer him to me . . . I did not give it a name, it was very difficult to understand. I knew there was something about me I could not label as such, you couldn't put a label on it and say this is me and this is why I am different. Quite frankly I should have known because a number of my friends in Lewisham Hospital were lesbians. I had spent the last couple of years in the hospital sharing a room with a woman who I knew subsequently to be a lesbian. It's not that we had a sexual relationship, we had a very great liking for each other. . . . And I think I myself was also under pressure at that time, and viewed marriage as a way of getting out of a situation that was very, very unpleasant. I was a nurse, I worked in Lewisham Hospital, we were constantly being bombed by V1s and V2s. We'd had direct hits, and we had a nation which was anti-German and which could not understand that I had refugee status. And with the pressure of treating victims of air raids and their facetious remarks all the time, the one thing I wanted to shed was my German nationality. The easiest way to do that was to marry somebody British. And it was that which attracted me at the time plus his rather pleasant personality, and his stance on the rights of human beings. We got married.

Many such marriages proved difficult or disastrous, especially when it came to sex. One way out was to try to commit suicide. By 1950 Sharley was a young mother with two small children:

Anything sexual I just couldn't stand, I felt nauseated. And it's difficult to explain; to me heterosexual sex was yucky, nasty, not natural, not for me. I just couldn't take this on board and I thought, Crikey, another forty years of that and I'll flip my lid. And the whole situation was very, very depressing at the time. I had kids, who I didn't particularly want to leave behind, but I attempted suicide. . . . I think the general stress of the situation had led up to it. We were poor, and after the war housing was terrible. We shared a house with my husband's brother-in-law and sister, not an ideal situation. They couldn't understand me and I couldn't really understand them – there was a block. And the general stresses of everyday life were colossal, plus this having to undergo something which felt to me like a torture. And I felt I just couldn't put up with it any longer. . . . I tried to commit suicide and I pre-meditated it. I sort of bought toys for my kids and I left a letter trying to explain, which was totally inadequate. I also realized I could not die at home because this would have been too much of a trauma. And I tried to rent a room somewhere but we were broke and I just didn't have the money. I found some bushes in Hyde Park which I knew very well and I thought I'll hide here. I had worked out in a rather logical way that if I gave myself a huge overdose of insulin, I would go into insulin shock if nobody found me and it would kill me. And in those days you could buy as much insulin as you wanted over the counter and you could also buy syringes. And that wasn't expensive. And the mistake I made was that I didn't realize the Hyde Park police went out on patrol in the park. They found me. And the first thing they gave me was strong tea, sugared tea, which counteracted the insulin immediately. I was extremely lucky that the policeman on duty was very, very sympathetic and talked to me like a Dutch uncle, and got in touch with my local police station. And I can remember being driven in a Black Maria to Shepherd's Bush and the Ealing police picking me up from there.

When a young person was discovered to have homosexual leanings there was an increasing likelihood that he or she would be referred to a doctor or hospital for an attempted cure. Traditionally, sodomy had been seen in terms of moral weakness and this view remained important in the medical profession until the inter-war years. However, coupled with the new concern with homosexuality from late Victorian times onwards went a more scientific approach to treating it. Essentially the new theories explained homosexuality in terms of hormonal or biological factors. One influential sexologist to popularize this view was Havelock Ellis. Although the more liberal books, like his on this subject, were sometimes banned – and when they were published many public libraries refused to display them – some editions filtered down to street level. They seem to have been a revelation to some of the confused and guilt-ridden homosexuals who stumbled across them for they were among the first modern books to propose that for some, homosexuality was a natural state of being. Paul Lanning:

And I didn't realize, I was too dim. I had a girlfriend in the village and I knew her for three years. We went out for walks together, and I did nothing physical in the way of an arm around the waist, nothing at all. When we said goodbye to each other she always said 'Paul, you're very cold, aren't you?' I didn't know what she meant, and I just laughed. I thought, 'Silly cow.' She was a lovely girl, a very fine girl, admirable in every way and she was very fond of me. And finally I wanted to leave my village because I was restricted there. I had ability and I studied the London matric. in the village. . . . And I came to London and it affected me immediately because, on a second-hand bookstall, I got a copy of Havelock Ellis's sexual psychology book number 6, and that explained everything immediately. I thought, 'That's me, I exist, I am a valid person.' Because I didn't even think I was a freak, I just thought I'd grow out of it. I realized I had problems but I didn't realize how different I was because I didn't know what homosexuality was. I knew that I existed. Havelock Ellis was a brilliant book for us.

Though liberating for some, most of the new theories and treatments for homosexuality were extremely repressive. Some homosexuals, for example, were put away in mental hospitals where they were subjected to everything from hypnotism to chemical experimentation. More often, they were referred by doctors to psychiatrists for counselling, and the advice was strongly laced with traditional prejudices. Bernard Williams was one of the ground staff working for Fighter Command during the Second World War:

> I suppose I had a kind of nervous breakdown and I was sent off to a pretty famous shrink who made a complete muck-up of the whole thing. He did discover I was homosexual as he described it. And he could cure my homosexuality. It was perfectly easy he said. I should find a nice girl, get married to her and I would be cured of these weirdo feelings that I'd got. Well, I know now that there was nothing wrong with me so there was nothing to be cured. But I did know a very nice girl – I've known lots and lots of girls – and we talked about it a lot, that I was homosexual. And we decided to risk the marriage.

Around the same time Dudley Cave received slightly more sympathetic treatment but it was of little practical use in his attempt to lead a new homosexual life:

British soldiers in drag perform a musical comedy in France in 1918. This kind of display was socially acceptable – especially in wartime – but any deviation from 'normal' sex roles in everyday life was very much taboo

It was not until I went into the army that I really came to grips with it. I decided, 'Right, I must do something.' I was a prisoner of war in the Far East and there had been a series of lectures on sex in the POW camp, not that it interested us very much because we were very badly undernourished and sexual urges died quickly. And the last one had a question time and lots of questions had been put in writing. At the end of it the medical officer said that a lot of the questions had been very personal and they'd arranged for a medical officer to be in the church every evening from six till seven and to go along and ask questions. Well, I walked up and down outside the church and went in and sat on a penitence bench with about seven or eight other people waiting to see the doctor. It was dark. When I got to the doctor I realized it was somebody I knew. It was an anaesthetist and he said, 'Hello Dudley, what's your trouble?' And I gulped and said, 'I'm homosexual.' And he said, 'Just because you masturbate it doesn't mean that.' And I must have said, 'Oh no, more than that,' in some sort of passion because he said, 'Look, don't go on. I'm not an expert in this field, but we have an expert in the camp and with your permission I'll refer you to him.' And he referred me to a very eminent sexologist Philip Bloom who happened to be a POW. He sort of straightened me out about it, told me that it appeared that I was, and not to worry about it. He lent me *Sexual Inversion in Men*, Havelock Ellis's book, to read. And I then began to understand. When I came out of the army I was a bit afraid of the costs of private medicine and I thought I might as well let the army sort out what I was going to do. So my final medical examination was by a red-faced senior officer. I sat down in front of him and he said, 'Well, you've been examined. Is there anything you need to tell us affecting your health?' And I said, 'Yes sir, I'm homosexual.' And he really went red in the face and a little vein in the side of his neck started throbbing and he was looking apoplectic. And in a rather choked voice he said, 'You'd better see a psychiatrist.' And he arranged for me to do so. Well, this rather worried me. In any case I eventually went to Millbank to see the psychiatrist. I saw him in a crowded room, where there were four psychiatrists and people zig-zagging all over the place, and I was extremely nervous and jumpy. And I told him my problem and he said 'I think we'd better admit you to hospital.' Well, this alarmed me dreadfully. What was I going to tell people? He said, 'Tell them you're very nervous and we think you ought to be checked up, that'll be all right.' Well, I was sent along to Sutton ENS hospital and arrived there on a Friday night, booked in, and I was left to sit around with a lot of quite badly disturbed people. The people at my dining table, four of them only had forks and spoons, they were not given knives. I saw a psychiatrist on the Monday morning and told him and he said 'Well, my advice to you

is that you should find somebody of like mind, settle down with
them and don't worry about it.' And he sent me home. Unfortunately he didn't tell me how to find somebody of like mind and it
was a long search. It took another ten years, I suppose.

Even when, in a minority of cases, sympathetic and intelligent advice
was given, the stigma attached to homosexuality and lesbianism made it
very difficult for most young people to accept their new sexual identity.
After failing to commit suicide Sharley McLaine was sent for psychia-
tric treatment.

I was extremely lucky in the psychiatrist I had who was a woman
and she came out one day and said to me, 'Well, you are a lesbian.'
I found that very hard to come to terms with. . . . That word in
those days, and I'm talking about 1950, had very, what shall I say,
nasty implications. I couldn't possibly be one of these women. It
was something I could not really accept in the beginning and you
find that's often true of a lot of us. We have a hard time coming to
terms with what we are, because we grow up in this society with all
its prejudices and they're passed on to us too. Homosexuality is
one of the areas where you listen to what other people say because
you never identify with it yourself, well I didn't anyway.

Sharley McLaine gradually accepted her lesbianism, she formed a
lasting relationship with another woman and 'came out' in the more
liberal atmosphere of the 1970s. For many years she has been a familiar
figure at Speakers' Corner in Hyde Park. Close to the spot where she
once tried to commit suicide she now campaigns every Sunday for
lesbian rights. Some of the homosexual men I interviewed like Dudley
Cave 'came out' and became active in the fight for Gay Rights in their
later years. They benefited from the openness, defiance and militancy
of the younger generation of homosexuals in the Gay Liberation
movement of the 1970s. The rejection of the word 'queer' and the
adoption of the more positive description 'gay' was one expression of
this new pride in the homosexual identity. Coupled with this development of a new gay culture and consciousness went a slightly more
relaxed attitude amongst heterosexuals towards homosexuality. The
prejudices and discrimination remain and still run deep. But those I
have spoken to have little doubt that the taboo of homosexuality is
nowhere near so powerful today as it was during the 1950s and before.

EPILOGUE:
THE END OF AN ERA?

In the 1950s the old era of Victorian condemnation of sex before marriage seemed to be coming to an end. The old taboos lost much of their former power. For the next quarter of a century more liberal attitudes towards young people and the sex life they chose for themselves were in the ascendant. This was the age of legalized abortions, the pill and homosexual law reform. The sexual liberation of the 1960s and 1970s broke the mould of the old morality. Although the influence of what came to be called the 'permissive society' has often been exaggerated, there is little doubt that it did bring in its wake important changes in the sexual behaviour of young people. Sex before marriage became more acceptable and more widespread than it had ever been since Victorian times. The rapid increase in the illegitimacy rate, the fall in the age of marriage and the widespread use of contraceptives among young people all point towards this. To some, it even seemed that this was the dawn of a new era of sexual freedom.

What changes there were took place against a background of economic prosperity, social reform and the development of the welfare state. In this more affluent age the rights and freedoms enjoyed by young people were considerably extended. The young often fought for their greater independence by defying old conventions or by political action through, for example, the Feminist and Gay Liberation movements. But one important reason why new rights were won was because many demands for change fitted the liberal direction in which British society was then moving. Basic welfare rights were granted to the single parent family (as the 'unmarried mother' came to be called), thus lifting one of the last great sanctions against sex before marriage. Sex education of a rudimentary kind was introduced into many schools and there was a boom in sex advice manuals which often encouraged the young to 'do their own thing'. Contraception and contraceptive advice were provided for young people and much of the stigma attached to treatments for sexual diseases was removed. Much sexual ignorance and anxiety remained of course – as survey after survey revealed. And sexual violence against women was heightened, partly as a result of the commercial exploitation of female sexuality which became a feature of the new liberal atmosphere. Nevertheless, traditional attitudes towards sexuality, especially those of a social purity type, seemed to be a thing of the past. Mary Whitehouse and the Festival of Light were, to many, dinosaurs in an age of sexual sophistication.

The 1980s have seen an unexpected sea change in the sexual

attitudes and behaviour of the young. The terror of AIDS, arriving with all the sudden drama of an Old Testament retribution, has begun to make sex before marriage far less fashionable and socially acceptable than it has been in recent decades. It is the latest in a procession of serious problems and panics – including broken homes, teenage pregnancies and rape – which have dented the liberal confidence of the permissive sixties. In today's uncertain atmosphere there has been a reassertion of traditional values. Some of the rights won in previous decades – for example, that of abortion for the single woman – are now under attack. And some of those who formed the rebellious younger generation of the 1960s ironically find themselves parents of children who have adopted the old sexual values that they rejected twenty-five years ago. The broader context within which this moral shift has occurred is one of economic recession, political conservatism and a popular crusade by Mrs Thatcher's government to re-establish Victorian values.

In this new moral climate there is a strong temptation to see the not so distant past as an age of lost innocence. Pre-war Britain – it is now sometimes claimed – was, compared to today, a safer and more contented place for young people to grow up to sexual maturity in. Most old people believe there were far fewer sexual problems in their day. But when we delve deeper into popular memory the stereotype of sexual respectability and rationality in the past begins to crack. Very often, just beneath the surface lie half forgotten, bitter-sweet memories of ignorance, fear and rebellion. For many, the taboo on sex before marriage had damaging and sometimes disastrous consequences. Young people lost control over an important part of their lives. Many unwanted pregnancies resulted. Couples married hastily, and sometimes unhappily, to avoid social disgrace. Gays and lesbians were forced to lead a double life which for the most part was one of isolation and despair. It was women far more than men who were the real victims of the sexual taboos of the time, and the greatest tragedy befell the unmarried mother. I have made a special effort in this book to try to rescue the stories of victims like these from obscurity and oblivion. It seems to me that their testimony is crucially important when making an assessment of sexual values past and present. Their memories make it clear that there was a high price to pay for the sexual respectability of the past – and part of the price was their lives.

FURTHER READING

Of the many books and articles I have read for this project, I found the following particularly useful and interesting:

1 Forbidden Fruit

Eustace Chesser, *The Sexual, Marital and Family Relationships of the English Woman* (Hutchinson, 1956); Eliot Slater and Moya Woodside, *Patterns of Marriage: A Study of Marital Relationships in the Urban Working Classes* (Cassell, 1951); Geoffrey Gorer, *Exploring English Character* (The Cresset Press, 1955); Mass Observation, *General Attitudes to Sex, 1949* (unpublished, Mass Observation Archive, University of Sussex); Jeffrey Weeks, *Sex, Politics and Society: The Regulation of Sexuality Since 1800* (Longman, 1981); John Springhall, *Coming of Age: Adolescence in Britain 1860–1960* (Gill and Macmillan, 1986); John Gillis, *Youth and History: Tradition and Change in European Age Relations 1770 to the Present* (Academic Press, 1974); Ruth Hall, *Dear Dr Stopes, Sex in the 1920s* (André Deutsch, 1979).

2 The Facts of Life

Edward Bristow, *Vice and Vigilance: Purity Movements in Britain Since 1700* (Gill and Macmillan, 1977); Alan Rusbridger, *History of the Sex Manual* (Faber, 1986); Peter Fryer, *The Birth Controllers* (Secker and Warburg, 1965); John Springhall, *Youth, Empire and Society* (Croom Helm, 1977); Michael Rosenthal, *The Character Factory: Baden-Powell and the Origins of the Boy Scout Movement* (Collins, 1986); John Burnett, *Destiny Obscure: Autobiographies of Childhood, Education and Family from the 1820s to the 1920s* (Penguin, 1984); Lesley Hall, 'Somehow Very Distasteful: Doctors, Men and Sexual Problems Between the Wars', in *Journal of Contemporary History*, Vol. 20, 1985.

3 The Road to Ruin

Peter Laslett (ed.) et al., *Bastardy and Its Comparative History* (Edward Arnold, 1980); Nigel Middleton, *When Family Failed* (Gollancz, 1971); John Francombe, *Abortion Freedom* (Allen and Unwin, 1984); Elaine Showalter, *The Female Malady: Women Madness and English Culture 1830–1980* (Virago, 1987); Susan Hartley, *Illegitimacy* (Berkeley, California, 1975); Christopher Smout, *A Century of the Scottish People* (Fontana, 1987); John Costello, *Love, Sex and War 1939–45* (Collins, 1985); Russell Davies, 'In a Broken Dream: Some Aspects of the Sexual Behaviour and Dilemmas of the Unmarried Mother in South

West Wales 1887–1914', in *Llafur* III (4), 1983, pp. 24–33; Andrew Scull (ed.), *Madhouses, Mad-doctors and Madmen: The Social History of Psychiatry in the Victorian Era* (Athlone Press, 1981); Andrew Blaikie, *Illegitimacy in Nineteenth Century North-East Scotland* (D. Phil., University of London, 1987).

4 Courtship Rituals
John Gillis, *For Better, For Worse: British Marriages 1600 to the Present* (Oxford University Press, 1985); Paul Thompson, *The Edwardians* (Paladin, 1977); Elizabeth Roberts, *A Woman's Place: An Oral History of Working-Class Women 1890–1940* (Blackwell, 1984); E. S. Turner, *A History of Courting* (Michael Joseph, 1954); Sylvana Tomaselli and Roy Porter (eds.), *Rape* (Blackwell, 1986).

5 Upstairs, Downstairs
Margaret Pringle, *Dance Little Ladies: The Days of the Debutante* (Orbis, 1977); John Gillis, 'Servants, Sexual Relations and the Risks of Illegitimacy in London 1801–1900', in *Feminist Studies* (Spring, 1979) pp. 142–73; Arthur Engel, 'Immortal Intentions: The University of Oxford and the Problem of Prostitution 1827–1914', in *Victorian Studies*, Vol. 23 no. 1 (Autumn, 1979) pp. 79–108; Jonathan Gathorne-Hardy, *The Public School Phenomenon 597–1977* (Hodder and Stoughton, 1977); Ian Gibson, *The English Vice: Beating, Sex and Shame in Victorian England and After* (Duckworth, 1978); Susan Edwards, *Female Sexuality and the Law* (Robertson, 1981).

6 Street Gang Sex
Geoff Pearson, *Hooligan: A History of Respectable Fears* (Macmillan, 1983); Clarence Rook, *The Hooligan Nights* (Oxford University Press, 1979, originally published 1899); Charles Russell, *Manchester Boys* (Manchester University Press, 1905); readers may also be interested in a previous book of mine which has a chapter on street gangs, *Hooligans or Rebels: An Oral History of Working Class Childhood and Youth 1889–1939* (Blackwell, 1981).

7 Beside the Sea
For an excellent introduction to the work of Mass Observation, see Dorothy Sheridan and Angus Calder, *Speak for Yourself: A Mass Observation Anthology* (Jonathan Cape, 1984). The Mass Observation quotes in this chapter are taken from this study. Also James Walvin, *Beside the Seaside: A Social History of the Popular Seaside Holiday* (Allen Lane, 1978); John Walton, *The English Seaside Resort: A Social History 1750–1914* (Leicester University Press, 1983).

8 The Other Love
Jeff Weeks, *Coming Out* (Quartet, 1977); H. Montgomery-Hyde, *The Other Love* (Mayflower, 1972); Annabel Farraday, *Social Definitions*

of Lesbians in Britain 1914–1939 (D. Phil., University of Essex, 1985).

Notes on interviewees

Most of the quotations in the book are from interviews by or correspondence with the author. Some were taken from the Family Life and Work Experience Archive at the University of Essex. The names – or pseudonyms – and the archive number of all the interview extracts used from this collection are as follows: Annie Ford, 143; Gladys Knight, 315; Joe Maddison, 155; Fred Mulligan, 140; Bill Reed, 249; Winnie Stradling, 230; Grace Sykes, 178; Frank Thomas, 380; Jane Thompson, 38; and Jack Woolf, 151. Betty Brown – another pseudonym – is interview no. 557 in the Manchester Studies collection held by the Documentary Photography Archive, Manchester. The extracts from the interviews with Lady Diana Cooper and Joyce Grenfell appeared in Margaret Pringle, *Dance Little Ladies: The Days of the Debutante* (Orbis, 1977).

Mass Observation Archive

One of the best primary sources for information on everyday life – including sex – in Britain, especially between the late 1930s and the early 1950s, is the Mass Observation Archive, University of Sussex Library. Contact the archivist, Dorothy Sheridan.

INDEX

Numbers in italics refer to illustrations